MW01381214

Gary Khan

GREATER

Don't Settle For Good When
There's Greater

©2021 Gary Khan
All rights reserved

CONTENTS

GREATER

"Considerably above the normal or average."

On a beautiful Southern California morning in July of 2021, I was having my morning devotions and praying through a list of needs that I have been asking God for regarding our church. As I was praying through my list I heard the Holy Spirit whisper, "You know you can ask for more."

I don't know about you, but I tend to not want to impose on the generosity of God. If I need $10, I ask for $10 not $100. But on that morning God was encouraging me, "You know you can ask for more. I have seen your heart and your motives, and I want you to ask for more."

There was more to that conversation, but the word that summed it all up was the word *"greater."* In his love and grace God wanted to give me greater provision, greater abundance, greater revelation, greater joy. You get the picture.

But I realized that word was not just for me. It is for you! God wants you, His people, to experience Greater.

He wants you to have greater intimacy, greater insight, greater increase, and greater influence. Good may be the enemy of great, but why settle for great when we can have Greater?

Some instructions...

This book was designed primarily as a 28-day devotional. Of course, you can make it a longer journey if you so desire. Sometimes I find that God wants me to camp out on something for a while so I can meditate on it and do the work of putting it into practice in my life. The primary desire in writing this devotional is for you to be transformed not just informed. I believe that transformation (becoming more and more like Jesus) is much more desirable than information (simply just knowing a bunch of stuff). At the end of the day, my prayer is that you will read the words and allow the Holy Spirit to work it into your life whether that takes 28 days or less...or more!

The layout is simple. There are entries for six of the seven days of the week. I have included the scripture passages at the beginning of each chapter so that you don't have to leave the book to read them, resist the urge to skip over them. Each day you read the entry I encourage you to read with pen in hand. Write in your book! This is something that you will come back to time after time. Underline, highlight, circle, color – whatever suits your fancy, as long as it contributes to active reading.

When you are done reading there are some questions for reflection and to move you to action. Don't just reflect...respond! Respond to the prompting of the Holy Spirit as He speaks to you each day. Write down what He is saying and what will you do about it. What will be your plan of action to go from information to transformation? This is where the real magic happens. Take your time, it is not a race to the finish but a journey with God as He works in us – enjoy the journey!

The seventh day is designed so that you can go back and review the previous six days and give God even more time to speak to you as you look at the week as a whole and not as singular entries. If you have ever watched something at a faster speed you will notice patterns that are missed when we are taking each day at a time. This weekly overview will allow for God to show you larger patterns or principles that you may have missed in the daily readings.

Let your goal be intimacy with God. Go for greater!

One last encouragement...

If you really want to take it up a notch, consider fasting during this time as you are going through this journal. You can go all biblical and abstain from all food (except water) for 28 days (I have done that before, and it is transformational). Okay, okay, hold on - don't quit reading, maybe you may want to take a more measured approach. Here are some tips for adding fasting to this challenge.

Week 1: Consider fasting TV and online media and spending the extra time reading God's Word.

Week 2: Fast a meal a day and use the time to read God's Word and pray.

Week 3: Consider doing a Daniel fast for the week. (For more info on a Daniel fast check out https://ultimatedanielfast.com)

Week 4: Continue with either the Daniel fast or fasting a meal a day, but maybe go without food for 24 hours or more. A lot of times I have ended with a 70-hour period of just water and spending extra time with God.

If you want more information on doing something more for fasting, there is a great booklet I have used called *7 Basic Steps to Successful Fasting & Prayer* by Bill Bright. You can purchase it on Amazon, or you can use this website: https://www.cru.org/us/en/train-and-grow/spiritual-growth/fasting/7-steps-to-fasting.html

greater intimacy

Chapter 1

I Want More!

(Anyone else hearing Ariel singing?)

Do you have any food you love to eat for which you don't have a cutoff switch? You can keep eating it and eating it and you want more and more. You go to bed thinking about it! You wake up thinking about it! When it comes to sweets, I don't have a cutoff switch. I just want more!

Have you ever eaten an entire bag of M&M's?
Or a whole tub of ice-cream?
How about $500.00 worth of sushi...and you still wanted more?

Do you ever feel that way about your relationship with God? You just can't get enough of God, you want more?

Now there are some side effects of wanting more and more of some foods, right? Increase! An increase of weight, cholesterol, blood pressure...you get the picture.

When it comes to God though, there are no bad side effects to having more – it's all good. More is better!

I am not sure that all of us will agree that more is better when it comes to serving Christ. I think that for many of us we are happy with the portion we have and don't want to get any more; it is good and that's that. When the Holy Spirit whispered to me on that summer morning, "You can ask for more," the word greater came to mind. I could have greater joy, greater peace, greater provision, greater power, greater things I will do in His name. The possibilities became infinitely greater, and I was filled with a sense of excitement of what was next – "I could have greater!"

"When it comes to God, there are no side effects to having more – it's all good. More is better!"

In keeping with my personality, I immediately started to ask myself some questions.

"Why am I settling for good enough?"

I think for me, I don't want to presume on God's goodness. I think that there is limit to His goodness. I don't want to be a pain in God's posterior; the whiny, needy kid that is never happy with what he has. I don't come out and say any of this because it sounds a little sacrilegious, but I unconsciously live it out, and I wonder if you can identify with that? Our actions point to a different set of beliefs than what we profess. Hmmm and ouch!

This begs another question – *"Does God feel that way about us asking Him?"*

He does not! The problem is that we have a wrong idea of who God is. We need to believe that He is good, that He is able and willing to do immeasurably more than we can ask or think, and that He loves us with a perfect love. He wants to give us more and He wants us to live in greater fullness.

Understanding that about God's nature and character, I must ask one more question…

Why do I want more?

Why do I want greater blessings, greater provision, greater power? Ahh, the issue of motivation! This is where the principle of Greater must first be grappled with.

Do I want more because I am selfish, and I am simply seeking the pursuit of happiness?

Do I want more because I believe that more things bring me joy and fulfillment?

Do I want more so I can feel superior?

OR…

Do I want more because I have discovered who God is and what He wants to do in and through me to accomplish His purposes, here on earth as it is in heaven?

I personally don't think that the answer is a clear cut either/or. I am human, therefore prone to selfishness. At the same time, I am a child of God and I have a desire to want more of Him.

For me, I see it as a sliding scale.

As I walk in relationship with God…

Am I becoming more and more motivated by who God is and what He wants to do in and through me?

Am I becoming less and less egocentric?

Do I want to do what He wants increasingly more than I want to do what I want?

As we begin a journey into greater, would you take some time to ask these questions and examine where you are and where you would like to be by the end of our time together?

- Am I settling for good enough? Why?
- What is my picture of God? Do I see Him as a good Father, do I see Him as a stingy, irritable boss, or...?
- Do I want more? Am I desperate for Greater?
- What is my motivation for the greater blessing? Do I want what is only in His hand or do I desire His heart?

Chapter 2

The Pathway To Greater

John 4:5–18 (NIV) [5] So he came to a town in Samaria called Sychar, near the plot of ground Jacob had given to his son Joseph. [6] Jacob's well was there, and Jesus, tired as he was from the journey, sat down by the well. It was about the sixth hour. [7] When a Samaritan woman came to draw water, Jesus said to her, "Will you give me a drink?" [8] (His disciples had gone into the town to buy food.) [9] The Samaritan woman said to him, "You are a Jew and I am a Samaritan woman. How can you ask me for a drink?" (For Jews do not associate with Samaritans.) [10] Jesus answered her, "If you knew the gift of God and who it is that asks you for a drink, you would have asked him and he would have given you living water." [11] "Sir," the woman said, "you have nothing to draw with and the well is deep. Where can you get this living water? [12] Are you greater than our father Jacob, who gave us the well and drank from it

himself, as did also his sons and his flocks and herds?" [13] *Jesus answered, "Everyone who drinks this water will be thirsty again,* [14] *but whoever drinks the water I give him will never thirst. Indeed, the water I give him will become in him a spring of water welling up to eternal life."* [15] *The woman said to him, "Sir, give me this water so that I won't get thirsty and have to keep coming here to draw water."* [16] *He told her, "Go, call your husband and come back."* [17] *"I have no husband," she replied. Jesus said to her, "You are right when you say you have no husband.* [18] *The fact is, you have had five husbands, and the man you now have is not your husband. What you have just said is quite true."*

The journey towards Greater must have a foundation – a starting point. That starting point for us is relationship. God invites us to relationship with Him because He, our Creator, knows that this is our deepest need and desire. The story of the woman at the well may seem random considering our context of "The Pathway to Greater," but bear with me for a second.

From the details the story reveals about her life choices, what would you say was her deepest desire? What was it that she was thirsty for?

The woman at the well desired relationship and looked for it in the arms of men. So deep was her longing that she was willing to break existing relationships to find "the relationship." I personally don't think that this is a bad approach at all, it was just misdirected. What she needed to find was the right relationship that would be worth it, and so far in her life she had not made the right relational decisions. All it had brought her was more emptiness and rejection. There is an old country song from the 80's that comes to mind every time I read this story (sung by Johnny Lee and written by Wanda Mallette, Bob Morrison and Patti Ryan)

Lookin' for love in all the wrong places
Lookin' for love in too many faces
Searchin' their eyes
Lookin' for traces
Of what I'm dreaming of…

"You can't have Greater if you don't have the right thing to start with."

That is exactly what this woman was doing, but then Jesus came along. He spoke to her deepest longing – He invited her to a relationship that would fill the cracks in her heart that nothing else was filling. Stop and think about it, in the culture of that time, it was a man that divorced a woman, and this woman had been divorced five times. She had been handed relational certificates of rejection at least five times. We can only imagine how that must have messed with her mind and emotions.

Deep within every one of us is a desire for relationship – but not just any relationship – we have a deep desire for a relationship with our Creator. That must be the starting point. The reality of pursuing Greater is that you can't have anything greater if you don't have the right thing to start with.

Where are you? Do you find yourself yearning for something that no other relationship in this world (with people or with things) can satisfy?

Every day you go through the motions, putting one foot in front of the other, making a living but feeling like you have no life.

You are desperate for something more; something that will fill the void.

Now, in the middle of going through the motions, Jesus slides up alongside of you and invites you to relationship with Him. Like the woman at the well, you are willing to break rules to seek fulfillment, so why not take another chance now and choose to come into relationship with Him? It is a choice that involves understanding and assenting to a few things...

- We accept the fact that we are born separated from God and cannot come back into relationship with Him on our own. The reason is because we are full of sin and that sin separates us from Him.
- But God wants us to have a relationship with Him, so He devised a plan that involved sending His Son Jesus, who came to earth as a sinless human being and who did what was necessary to pay the penalty for our sins.
- Now, anyone who wants to come into relationship with God can do so by believing in Jesus as God's Son and our Savior and asking God to forgive us of our sins. It is as simple as that.

Why not make that decision today?

The decision to pursue relationship with God the Father is worth it! You simply choose to believe in Jesus as the Son of God and the One who saves you from sin, and then ask Him to forgive you of your sins. When you believe and ask, it is done in an instant. Kapow! Voilà! Or as one of my daughters says, "Bling Blaou!"

Maybe you are reading this, and you have already made that decision, then take a moment to re-affirm it to yourself and God. Consider re-affirming this with communion. Don't neglect to do this just because you don't have grape juice and crackers, use whatever is available in this moment. If you are having your quiet time with a cup of coffee and toast, then use those as the elements to remember Jesus' act of providing salvation for us.

You may also consider praying for two or three of your friends or family members who you would like to see come into relationship with God.

Chapter 3

Good is the Enemy of Greater

Genesis 11:31 (NIV) *Terah took his son Abram, his grandson Lot son of Haran, and his daughter-in-law Sarai, the wife of his son Abram, and together they set out from Ur of the Chaldeans to go to Canaan. But when they came to Haran, <u>they settled there</u>.*

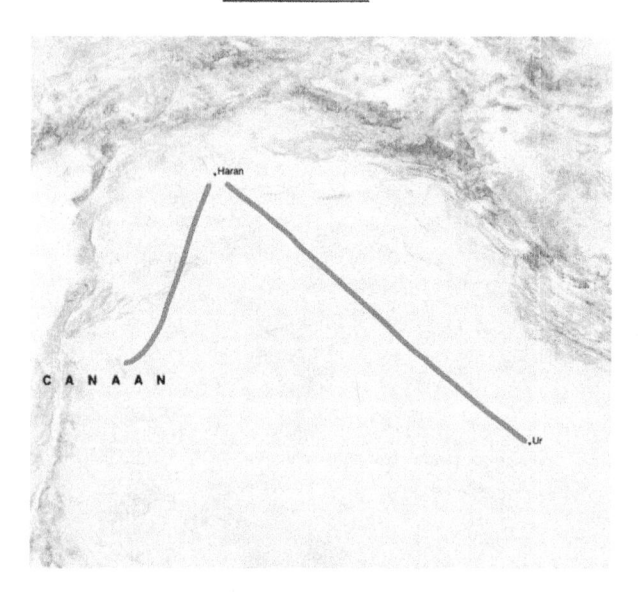

If you read that verse correctly you would have burst into tears immediately – it is one of the saddest verses in the Bible, and what makes it even sadder is that this really is the story of so many others as well.

A couple of questions for you to ponder.

- Where was their final destination?
- Where did they settle?

Abraham and his group were traveling with lots of people and livestock in their caravan. Haran seemed like a good rest stop. We could take a potty break, fill up the camels and everyone could catch up on their eating.

"It was a fertile area and good for grazing."

So, they stayed a while and that while turned into a lifestyle. They stopped halfway! I wonder if that may seem familiar? How many times have we stopped at a "rest-stop" along the way and ended up staying there?

My dad would repetitively say to me, "Son, good is the enemy of great!" but I think I want to change that to "Good is the enemy of Greater!" Nowhere is that truer than in our relationship with God. A lot of people begin a relationship with God, but they never go for the greater relationship – they settle on the outskirts, or halfway from the real thing and seem comfortable to get a shadow of the real thing.

Which would you prefer?
$1000 or $1,000,000?
Half a car or a whole car?

Are you settling for good enough when God invites you to Greater?

Are you content with a relationship with God that I call the "spare tire" relationship? You go along on your own until you run into a rough patch and get a flat. That is when you pull God out from the trunk and use Him till you can get things repaired and running again. There is something greater to be experienced!

Are you the more along the lines of the "Christian wear" relationship? You talk about God, and you have all the Christian accoutrements, but it is all on a surface level – it has not reached to the deepest, innermost parts of your life. There is something greater to be experienced!

> ***1 Corinthians 2:9 (TPT)*** [9] *...Things never discovered or heard of before, things beyond our ability to imagine — these are the many things God has in store for all his lovers.*

"Don't settle! Go for Greater!"

Have you stopped for a break and have not gotten back on the journey?

In what areas of your walk with God are you settling for good instead of great?

What are you going to do about it? Come up with a plan of action to get back on the road again.

Chapter 4

Desire

"God, I want to know you more!"

Psalm 42:1-2 (TPT) I long to drink of you, O God,
to drink deeply from the streams of pleasure
flowing from your presence.
My longings overwhelm me for more of you!
2 My soul thirsts, pants,
and longs for the living God.
I want to come and see the face of God.

1 Corinthians 9:24–27 (NLT) 24 Don't you realize
that in a race everyone runs, but only one person
gets the prize? So run to win! 25 All athletes are
disciplined in their training. They do it to win a
prize that will fade away, but we do it for an
eternal prize. 26 So I run with purpose in every
step. I am not just shadowboxing. 27 I discipline

my body like an athlete, training it to do what it should. Otherwise, I fear that after preaching to others I myself might be disqualified.

Philippians 3:7–8 (NIV) [7] *But whatever was to my profit I now consider loss for the sake of Christ.* [8] *What is more, I consider everything a loss compared to the surpassing greatness of knowing Christ Jesus my Lord, for whose sake I have lost all things. I consider them rubbish, that I may gain Christ.*

What do these verses have in common?

They all speak of a deep desire, a craving. It is not the take it or leave kind of desire. Nope, this is the drug-addict-craving-a-hit kind of desire. This is the young lover pining for her beloved kind of desire. This is the gold medal or bust Olympian kind of pursuit.

> *"Our journey with Christ is an invitation to desire. Yet, when measuring spiritual health, we usually ask questions about duty and doctrine: Am I doing the right things? Am I willing to sign this statement of faith?"*
> Matthew Woodley

If we are to not settle for less than, then there needs to be a desire burning within us – the desire to want to know God in greater intimacy. Discipline and duty are necessary. But if they are the primary motivators for Greater, then what we will encounter is drudgery. The desire for intimacy is the motivation that moves us. It pulls us out of the rest stops and gets us back on the road towards greater.

Saint Augustine of Hippo **in *The Confessions of St. Augustine*** gives us a taste of the desire for greater intimacy...

> Late have I loved you, beauty so old and so new: late have I loved you. ... You were fragrant, and I drew in my breath and now pant after you. I tasted you, and I feel but hunger and thirst for you. You touched me, and I am set on fire to attain the peace which is yours. [1]

> ***Matthew 14:22–29 (NIV)*** [22] *Immediately Jesus made the disciples get into the boat and go on ahead of him to the other side, while he dismissed the crowd.* [23] *After he had dismissed them, he went up on a mountainside by himself to pray. When evening came, he was there alone,* [24] *but the boat was already a considerable distance from land, buffeted by the waves because the wind was against it.* [25] *During the fourth watch of the night Jesus went out to them, walking on the lake.* [26] *When the disciples saw him walking on the lake, they were terrified. "It's a ghost," they said, and cried out in fear.* [27] *But Jesus immediately said to them: "Take courage! It is I. Don't be afraid."* [28] *"Lord, if it's you," Peter replied, "tell me to come to you on the water."* [29] *"Come," he said. Then Peter got down out of the boat, walked on the water and came toward Jesus.*

---

[1] **Confessions Oxford World Classics** Translated by Henry Chadwick (2009)

This is one of my favorite stories in the Bible. I must admit that I give Peter a bad rap because in the middle of the miracle he gets scared, but let's look at this from a little different perspective for a moment.

The 12 disciples are in the boat going over to the other side of the lake as Jesus had commanded them to. It's business as usual. They had just been with Him and now they were going to meet Him on the other side. Halfway through the journey, the storm kicks up and they are having a tough go of it trying to get to where Jesus told them to be. In the middle of all of this, things get a little stranger when they see a ghost walking on the water. It turns out that it is Jesus taking a casual stroll in the early morning hours through storm-tossed waters. He calls out to them and tells them not to worry,

"Hey yawl, it's just little ole me walking on water. Stay calm and carry on." (You might want to read that with a drawl.)

Here is where I love Peter's heart. He had just been with Jesus a few hours earlier, but now when he sees Jesus, he does not respond like the rest of the guys in the boat,
"Oh okay, Jesus is over there, cool."
Instead, Peter pursues Jesus. He is not satisfied to see Jesus from afar, he does what none of the other disciples did, he calls out to Jesus,
"Jesus, I want to come closer to you. Tell me to come, please! Please? I want to come near to You!"

And Jesus invites him to come nearer.

If I were the disciples, I would think that Peter was being a little overdramatic.

"Brown-noser!"

"Come on, we just saw Jesus a few hours ago and now He is right over there."

"Relax, we will be near Him again soon enough."
But Peter was not satisfied with that – he wanted Greater. So, he calls out to Jesus,

"Can I come to You?"
Jesus invites him to come. Peter ignores the rolling of the eyes and the snide comments from the other disciples. He braves the storm and steps out of the boat into a roiling lake and begins his trek toward Jesus.

We all know what happens next – he falters. He gets scared halfway there and Jesus had to rescue him. The guys in the boat are laughing and he knows he is not going to hear the end of this. In the middle of a disagreement they will be having on the road someday, one of them will start play acting,

"Jesus, please help little ole me, I'm drowning! Glug, glug."

But whatever you do, don't feel bad for Peter. Think about it – he may have faltered and had to be rescued, but he still ended up closer to Jesus than any of the others, and he is the only person, other than Jesus, to have walked on water! If that is failure, then I want more! His desire to be with Jesus motivated him to want more and allowed him a greater revelation of Jesus.

Later in his life he gives us a glimpse of that same kind of desire and passion when he encourages…

>**1 Peter 2:2 (NLT)** *² Like newborn babies, you must
>underline crave pure spiritual milk so that you will grow into
>a full experience of salvation. Cry out for this
>nourishment…*

What would you do to have greater intimacy with God?

Who and what are you willing to leave behind for it?

Here are some ideas.

> ***Mark 10:17–21 (TPT)*** *¹⁷ As Jesus started on his way, a man came running up to him. Kneeling down in front of him, he cried out, "Good Teacher, what one thing am I required to do to gain eternal life?" ¹⁸ Jesus responded, "Why do you call me good? Only God is truly good. ¹⁹ You already know the commandments: 'Do not murder, do not commit adultery, do not steal, do not give a false testimony, do not cheat, and honor your father and mother.' " ²⁰ The man said to Jesus, "Teacher, I have carefully obeyed these laws since my youth." ²¹ Jesus fixed his gaze upon the man, with tender love, and said to him, "Yet there is still one thing in you lacking. Go, sell all that you have and give the money to the poor. Then all of your treasure will be in heaven. After you've done this, come back and walk with me."*

__Luke 14:25–27 (TPT)__ [25] As massive crowds followed Jesus, he turned to them and said, [26] "When you follow me as my disciple, you must put aside your father, your mother, your wife, your sisters, your brothers—yes, you will even seem as though you hate your own life. This is the price you'll pay to be considered one of my followers. [27] And anyone who comes to me must be willing to share my cross and experience it as his own, or he cannot be considered to be my disciple.

Chapter 5

Devotion
"God, I will seek You!"

Psalm 63:1 (NIV) [1] O God, you are my God, earnestly I seek you; my soul thirsts for you, my body longs for you, in a dry and weary land where there is no water.

Acts 2:41–42 (NLT) [41] Those who believed what Peter said were baptized and added to the church that day—about 3,000 in all. [42] All the believers devoted themselves to the apostles' teaching, and to fellowship, and to sharing in meals (including the Lord's Supper), and to prayer.

Greater intimacy requires devotion. A dedication to seek God earnestly. But how exactly can we do that? What does that even look like in practical terms and not just the passionate uttering of words? Acts 2 gives us some practical insight.

Peter gets up and preaches to a group of people and three thousand people were born into the family of God. Amazing! But, as we have talked about, this is only the first step of the journey towards Greater.

The three thousand have come into relationship with God through His Son Jesus, and now there is a burning desire to grow in greater relationship with Him, so they...

- *devoted* themselves to learning more about what God's Word required of them,
- *committed themselves* to living in deep fellowship with the community of believers
- *dedicated themselves* to eating together and remembering what Jesus did for them
- *gave themselves fully* to the prayers.

If desire is what fuels us, then devotion to these simple things is the vehicle that can get us there.

"If desire is what fuels us, then devotion (to God's Word, deep fellowship, communion and prayer) is the vehicle that can lead us into intimacy."

On the journey to Greater we need to be taught how to live according to God's ways. God has given apostles, prophets, pastors, teachers, and evangelists to teach us these things and we must choose to be committed to this process. (Ephesians 4:10-16) This idea of being taught is not just the transferring of information but it is the idea of information that requires a response. God's appointed leaders in the church are given to equip God's people – that means they teach you the principles and then hold you accountable for putting those principles into action. Don't be upset when they are living true to their calling, be thankful and be responsive to them – they are teaching you to obey everything that Jesus has commanded.

Left to pursue intimacy on our own we tend to falter, and our passion tends to wane. We get distracted and start pursuing peripheral or non-essential things. This is why one of the things we must devote ourselves to, if we want to experience the greater, is Christian fellowship – living in the community of believers. In Christian community we "spur one another on towards love and good deeds." We find that community sharpens us as we encourage one another and strengthen each other. We need to remember that Christian community is a spiritual weapon that we must use to counter the attack of the enemy.

A commitment to the sacrament of communion reminds us of who Jesus is and what He has done on our behalf. We are reminded of our absolute need for Him and that deepens our hunger and thirst for Him.

Devoting ourselves to prayer is so vital as prayer is direct communication with God. If you want to develop intimacy and deepen relationship then regular, honest, and unfiltered two-way communication is necessary.

- Are you devoting yourself to these things?
- Which one needs attention?
- Create a plan of action to be devoted to it.
- Who will you ask to keep you honest in your devotion?

Chapter 6

Discipline
"God I will stay!"

Exodus 33:7–11 (The Message) [7] *Moses used to take the Tent and set it up outside the camp, some distance away. He called it the Tent of Meeting. Anyone who sought GOD would go to the Tent of Meeting outside the camp.* [8] *It went like this: When Moses would go to the Tent, all the people would stand at attention; each man would take his position at the entrance to his tent with his eyes on Moses until he entered the Tent;* [9] *whenever Moses entered the Tent, the Pillar of Cloud descended to the entrance to the Tent and GOD spoke with Moses.* [10] *All the people would see the Pillar of Cloud at the entrance to the Tent, stand at attention, and then bow down in worship, each man at the entrance to his tent.* [11] *And GOD spoke with Moses face-to-face, as neighbors speak to one another. When he would*

return to the camp, his attendant, the young man
Joshua, stayed—he didn't leave the Tent.

There are three different people represented in this story.

The Israelites

They were known as the people of God, but their relationship was summed up in being content to worship God from afar. God was real and desired relationship with them, but they were satisfied to watch from the shadow of their tents. He resided outside of their everyday living spaces. He was not the center of their lives but a separate category. The Israelites were happy to let someone else meet with God on their behalf. Verse seven informs us that anyone who sought God (or desired to seek God) would go to the Tent of Meeting outside the camp...yet none of them went. They had access but they didn't have desire or the discipline to do it.

Moses

Moses took the extra walk to the tent of meeting because of desire, devotion, and duty. As a leader, he needed to seek God for direction in how to lead His people. He needed God's help and he knew it, so he sought God. God showed up and spoke face to face with him, as one friend to another. What a beautiful picture, one that I long for and pursue. I want to be a friend of God.

Joshua

Joshua went because he was Moses' assistant. He went out of duty – and he experienced the presence of God because he was with Moses. [Good lesson to glean right there huh? The people you hang out with rub off on you.] Joshua got all the joy of presence because of his relationship with Moses. But Joshua did not content himself with that (and he could have), he wanted more! So, when Moses left, Joshua stayed. He pursued God further. He was not content to live off Moses' blessings – he wanted his own and he wanted Greater.

Joshua pushed his way through, he didn't just stay at the entrance of the tent – he went in. And having gained access to God's presence he stayed; he refused to leave. He possessed desire, devotion, discipline, and duty – and God gave him more.

Are you lingering in the "tent" with God?

Who are you most like in the story? Who would you like to be?

So often we are being pulled in many different directions and usually the first thing to suffer is our time in the tent. God has made it so much easier as well, we don't have to go to a physical tent, He is always near to us. Will you take time to spend time with Him and if you want greater – will you stay a while?

Consider creating a playlist of a few songs that help you focus on staying in the tent. I have one that lasts about 30-60 minutes that I will play and then spend time just being in the tent.

I don't have to talk the whole time. I simply start by asking God what is on His heart that He would like to reveal to me. When I hear from Him, I start asking questions for greater revelation and understanding. Try it!

Chapter 7

Doing

Spend time today just continuing to pursue intimacy with God. This is the foundation for everything greater that God wants to do in you and through you. Practice what you did yesterday.

Go to a place where you can have uninterrupted time. Go sit in the park, take a long and leisurely walk, wake up early before everyone else and sit in the living room alone...

Ask God to speak to you.

Father what is on Your heart?

How would you like me to pray?

For whom do you want me to pray?

Then spend time listening and responding.

Write down anything you feel that God is speaking to you. If it requires action on your part, then what is your next step?

Sometimes it helps me to structure the time by praying ACTS.

- Adoration
- Confession
- Thanksgiving
- Supplication – my prayer requests.

Whatever you do, the goal is to draw near to God. To seek Him, to allow Him to reveal Himself to you, to give Him unhindered and unhurried time.

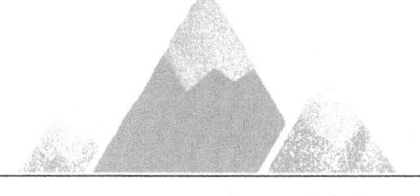

greater insight

Invitation followed by obedience leads to intimacy.
Intimacy leads to revelation.
Revelation leads to greater invitation.

Chapter 8

Intimacy Leads To Revelation

Exodus 3:1–4:17 (NIV) [1] *Now Moses was tending the flock of Jethro his father-in-law, the priest of Midian, and he led the flock to the far side of the desert and came to Horeb, the mountain of God.* [2] *There the angel of the LORD appeared to him in flames of fire from within a bush. Moses saw that though the bush was on fire it did not burn up.* [3] *So Moses thought, "I will go over and see this strange sight—why the bush does not burn up."* [4] *When the LORD saw that he had gone over to look, God called to him from within the bush, "Moses! Moses!" And Moses said, "Here I am."* [5] *"Do not come any closer," God said. "Take off your sandals, for the place where you are standing is holy ground."* [6] *Then he said, "I am the God of your father, the God of Abraham, the God of Isaac and the God of Jacob." At this, Moses hid his face, because he was afraid to look at God.* [7] *The LORD said, "I have indeed seen the misery of my people in Egypt. I have heard them crying out*

because of their slave drivers, and I am concerned about their suffering. [8] So I have come down to rescue them from the hand of the Egyptians and to bring them up out of that land into a good and spacious land, a land flowing with milk and honey... [10] So now, go. I am sending you to Pharaoh to bring my people the Israelites out of Egypt." [11] But Moses said to God, "Who am I, that I should go to Pharaoh and bring the Israelites out of Egypt?" [12] And God said, "I will be with you. And this will be the sign to you that it is I who have sent you: When you have brought the people out of Egypt, you will worship God on this mountain." [13] Moses said to God, "Suppose I go to the Israelites and say to them, 'The God of your fathers has sent me to you,' and they ask me, 'What is his name?' Then what shall I tell them?" [14] God said to Moses, "I AM WHO I AM. This is what you are to say to the Israelites: 'I AM has sent me to you.'" [15] God also said to Moses, "Say to the Israelites, 'The LORD, the God of your fathers—the God of Abraham, the God of Isaac and the God of Jacob—has sent me to you.' This is my name forever, the name by which I am to be remembered from generation to generation. [16]

"Go, assemble the elders of Israel and say to them, 'The LORD, the God of your fathers—the God of Abraham, Isaac and Jacob— appeared to me and said: I have watched over you and have seen what has been done to you in Egypt. [17] And I have promised to bring you up out of your misery in Egypt ...a land flowing with milk and honey... [1] Moses answered, "What if they do not believe me or listen to me and say, 'The LORD did not appear to you'?" [2] Then the LORD said to him, "What is that in your hand?" "A staff," he replied. [3] The LORD said, "Throw it on the ground." Moses threw it on the ground and it became a snake, and he ran from it. [4] Then the LORD said to him, "Reach out your hand and take it by the tail." So Moses reached out and took hold of the snake and it turned back into a staff in his hand. [5] "This," said the LORD, "is so that they may believe that the LORD, the God of their fathers—the God of Abraham, the God of Isaac and the God of Jacob—has appeared to you." [6] Then the LORD said, "Put your hand inside your cloak." So Moses put his hand into his cloak, and when he took it out, it was leprous, like snow. [7] "Now put it back into your cloak," he said. So Moses put his hand back into his cloak, and when he took it out, it was restored, like the rest of his flesh. [8] Then the LORD said, "If they do not believe you or pay attention to the first miraculous sign, they may believe the second. [9] But if they do not believe these two signs or listen to you, take some water from the Nile and pour it on the dry ground. The water you take from the river will become blood on the ground." [10] Moses said to the LORD, "O Lord, I have never been eloquent, neither in the past nor since you have spoken to your servant. I am slow of speech and tongue." [11] The LORD said to him, "Who gave man his mouth? Who makes him deaf or mute? Who gives him sight or makes him blind? Is it not I, the LORD? [12] Now go; I will help you speak and will teach you what to say." [13] But Moses said, "O Lord, please send someone else to do it." [14] Then the LORD's anger burned against Moses and he said, "What about your brother, Aaron the Levite? I know he can speak

well. He is already on his way to meet you, and
his heart will be glad when he sees you. [15] You
shall speak to him and put words in his mouth; I
will help both of you speak and will teach you
what to do. [16] He will speak to the people for you,
and it will be as if he were your mouth and as if
you were God to him. [17] But take this staff in your
hand so you can perform miraculous signs with
it."

Moses goes to "the mountain of the Lord" – a place that signified the presence of the Lord. During the course of his workday, Moses goes where he knows God is to be found. While he is there he comes across a strange sight – a bush burning but not being burned up. It was God inviting Moses to draw nearer. Moses could have enjoyed the sight and gone on his way, but he desired the greater, so when God spoke to him to come nearer – he obeyed. He didn't make up excuses about being busy or wondering who would take care of the sheep – he responded in obedience to the invitation of God.

Invitation followed by obedience leads to intimacy.
Intimacy leads to revelation.
Revelation leads to greater invitation.

When he drew near, God began to pour out revelation to Moses. Here are some of the things that we see God revealing in that moment when Moses chose intimacy.
- God revealed His plan and purpose for Moses.
- Moses begins to converse with God and asks a lot of questions. "I don't think I am qualified enough. God, I don't have the right gifting. No one will listen."

- God reveals His answers to Moses' questions and concerns. He assures him that He is in it, and He will provide all that Moses needs to accomplish what God had called him to do.
- God also revealed His name to Moses – I AM WHO I AM! I am the Eternal One. I was, I am and always will be!

God has so much He wants to reveal to us. He has a plan and purpose for your life that is greater than anything that you can imagine or dream of. He wants to let us in on His plans, but it starts with intimacy. "God, I want to know you. God, I will earnestly seek You. God, I want more of You so I will stay in Your presence when everyone else walks away. I will draw near to You!"

When we do those things, we begin to experience a greater revelation of God. That day God gave Moses a deeper glimpse of who He was – not just the God of Abraham, Isaac, and Jacob – but the Eternal One. The God of Moses too.

God wants to give you a greater revelation of Himself and His unfolding plan. He wants to appear to you, appoint you, anoint you and answer all your concerns. Here is the crazy thing, Greater is not a one and done deal.
- Invitation followed by obedience leads to intimacy.
- Intimacy leads to revelation.
- Revelation leads to greater invitation.
- Greater invitation followed by greater obedience leads to greater intimacy.
- Greater intimacy leads to greater revelation...

The bush is burning, the tent is open, the invitation has been issued – come and experience Greater!

Where are you right now in this process? Invitation, obedience, intimacy, revelation? What do you need to do to get to the next step?

What things are keeping you from greater intimacy?

Chapter 9

A Revelation of His Goodness

Luke 18:19 (NIV) [19] *...Jesus answered. "No one is good—except God alone.*

1 John 1:5 (TPT) [5] *This is the life-giving message we heard him share and it's still ringing in our ears. We now repeat his words to you: God is pure light. You will never find even a trace of darkness in him.*

Psalm 119:68 (NIV) [68] *You are good, and what you do is good;*

Psalm 100:5 (NIV) [5] *For the LORD is good and his love endures forever; his faithfulness continues through all generations.*

How do we measure goodness?

In order to measure something, we need a standard that it is compared to. 20 pounds are so declared because there is a standard of measurement for a pound. So, what is the standard with which we measure goodness? The standard is God! He is holy – without any sin. He is righteous – whatever He does is right, so He is the measure of what is good.

What can you glean from the verses above regarding God's goodness?

When we say He is good…
It means that there is no evil to be found in Him.
It means that He does what is right and His intentions are not self-serving because it is based on a deep and selfless love.
Whatever the outcome of His plans they can be trusted as good.

> **James 1:17 (TPT)** [17] *Every gift God freely gives us is good and perfect, streaming down from the Father of lights, who shines from the heavens with no hidden shadow or darkness and is never subject to change.*

> **Romans 8:27–28 (TPT)** [27] *God, the searcher of the heart, knows fully our longings, yet he also understands the desires of the Spirit, because the Holy Spirit passionately pleads before God for us, his holy ones, in perfect harmony with God's plan and our destiny.* [28] *So we are convinced that every detail of our lives is continually woven together to fit into God's perfect plan of bringing good into our lives, for we are his lovers who have been called to fulfill his designed purpose.*

Say it out loud! *"God You are good! In you there is no darkness or evil! In you there is perfect love! All that You do is good!"*

In Genesis chapters 37 – 50 we find the story of Joseph. Here is a quick synopsis.

Joseph is the favorite of Jacob's eleven sons. This leads to a little bit of sibling jealously. So much so that the ten other brothers conspire to kill Joseph. Yikes! That is some serious jealously! At the last minute they decide not to kill him but to sell him off as a slave, how magnanimous of them right?! Now I don't know about you, but if I am Joseph, I am not thinking that this was a better deal – I think it would have been more humane to kill him, but they don't.

"Everything that God does is good!"

In the ensuing years, Joseph's life has more emotional ups and downs than watching a seal being chased by a great white during Shark Week. (Out of curiosity, who are you rooting for?) He finds favor, he falls out of favor. He finds favor, he falls out of favor. He finds favor...you get the idea. Yet through it all Joseph does not falter in his love and devotion for God. Then one day, seemingly out of the blue, without any warning, he is elevated from living in prison to ruling in the palace of the greatest empire at that time – Egypt. He is second in command to the Pharaoh himself. Now that's a great ending, except it is not the ending.

Through a series of "coincidences" there comes a day when the brothers, who had betrayed him so long ago when they sold him into slavery, show up at the palace. They are there to ask Joseph to be merciful to them and give them food. They don't even recognize Joseph, but he recognizes them immediately. He decides to have a little fun at their expense and then after he messes with them a bit, he reveals himself to them. Right about this time the brothers are soiling their underwraps. They know what they have done, and they are thinking about how they would respond if they were given the chance to exact revenge. I so love Joseph's response to his brothers though,

> ***Genesis 50:19–20 (NIV)*** *¹⁹ But Joseph said to them, "Don't be afraid. Am I in the place of God? ²⁰ You intended to harm me, but God intended it for good to accomplish what is now being done, the saving of many lives.*

In my paraphrase Joseph says,

"Bros don't sweat it! It's all good. You may have intended to take me down, but God didn't count me out because He intended it for something good. He is good and all that He does is good. His intentions are not self-serving because it is based on a deep and selfless love for me, for you and so many others! I'm only going to mess with you for a little bit."

"All that God does is good!"

You want Greater? Then we need to really embrace this. "All that God does is good!" If we believe that God is good and all that He does is good, then we experience the greater life in Him when we live with thankfulness and a firm conviction that every detail of our lives is continually woven together to fit into God's perfect plan of bringing good into our lives and the lives of so many others!

A Revelation of His Goodness

What are the areas of your life that you need to apply this truth to so you can live in the Greater?

In what ways can you imitate this characteristic of God's goodness into your own life?

Take some time to read Psalm 107 out loud.

Chapter 10

A Revelation of His Power

Jeremiah 32:17 (NIV) [17] *"Ah, Sovereign LORD, you have made the heavens and the earth by your great power and outstretched arm. Nothing is too hard for you.*

Luke 1:37 (TPT) [37] *Not one promise from God is empty of power, for nothing is impossible with God!"*

Ephesians 3:20 (TPT) [20] *Never doubt God's mighty power to work in you and accomplish all this. He will achieve infinitely more than your greatest request, your most unbelievable dream, and exceed your wildest imagination! He will outdo them all, for his miraculous power constantly energizes you.*

God is omnipotent – which means that He is all powerful. A better way to say it, in my opinion, is to say that there are no limits to what He can do. Theologian Wayne Grudem says that *"there are no external constraints on what God can do and He has the power to do all that He decides to do."*[2]

In **Numbers 13 and 14** we read the story of the twelve spies who were tasked with scouting out the land of Canaan. It was a simple directive to go and see...

What the land is like? Is it good or bad?

What kind of towns do the people live in? Are they unwalled or fortified?

How is the soil? Is it fertile or poor? Are there trees on it or not?

Are the people who live there are strong or weak; few or many?

Do your best to bring back some of the fruit of the land.

After 40 days of scoping out the land that the people of Israel had been dreaming about for 400 plus years, they come back. I can just imagine it. They walk in with a cluster of grapes so big that two guys had to carry it. The other ten were loaded down with juicy pomegranates and sweet, luscious figs.

The people are crowding around and eager to hear their report.

"What is the land like? Is it good, and is the soil good?"

"The land is unbelievable. The soil is rich and fertile. Check out the fruit we brough back, they are amazing, **but**

---

[2] Grudem, W. A. (2004). **Systematic theology: An introduction to Biblical Doctrine** (p. 197). Leicester, England; Grand Rapids, MI: Inter-Varsity Press; Zondervan Pub. House.

we will really have to work to get the fruit, it's not like getting manna every day."

"Are the people who live there are strong or weak, few or many?" The people ask.

"The land is overflowing with blessings, **but** the people there are powerful, and they live in fortified cities, and they are waaaaay bigger than we can imagine – they are giants! We are screwed!"

"Ahhhh! Why is God doing this to us?" The people start complaining.

"Hang on to your pomegranates everyone, we can do this!" Caleb (one of the spies) shouts.

"Why did God mess with us like this? And who is the idiot that brought us here? Let's find a new leader and go back into slavery." The people all say. (Did we really just hear them say that? Sounds ridiculous right? Slavery is better than freedom?)

"Wait everyone, the land we passed through and explored is exceptionally good. **God will** lead us into that land, a land flowing with milk and honey, and **He will give it to us**." Moses counters.

"No word from God is without the inherent power to accomplish it."

Do you see how our big buts get us in trouble? The ten spies were like, "We liiike big buts and we cannot lie..."

They kept on going...

"It is everything God has promised us **but** there is no way we are going to get it. God is just teasing us – there is no way we can get it because we are not strong enough. There are giants in the land!"

They saw the giants and forgot something of greater importance, that the land was promised to them by God and

God is powerful – able to do what He determines to do. Long before the spies went to scope out the land, God had told them that He was the One who would deliver them into the land…

> *Exodus 33:1–3 (NIV)* [1] *Then the LORD said to Moses, "Leave this place, you and the people you brought up out of Egypt, and go up to the land I promised on oath to Abraham, Isaac and Jacob, saying, 'I **will give** it to your descendants.'* [2] *I **will send** an angel before you and drive out the Canaanites, Amorites, Hittites, Perizzites, Hivites and Jebusites.* [3] *[All you need to do is just] Go up to the land flowing with milk and honey…"*

God promised, and no word from God is without the inherent power to accomplish it!

He was the One who had assumed responsibility for bringing them into the land, all they had to do was trust and obey. If God willed it, then He would make a way. Their despair showed their unbelief in the power of God.

So often we say that God is powerful – able to do all that He determines to do – but when the situations and circumstances threaten to overcome us, we give up in despair and we miss out on the things that God had purposed to bless us with. Of the twelve men who went to spy out the land, only two believed in the power of God to accomplish what He had promised. And only these two, Joshua and Caleb, got to experience the blessings of God.

Yes, there were giants in the land that needed to be conquered.

Yes, it was not going to be a plug and play, instantaneous result.

What the ten spies did is what a lot of us do, we forget that many times, the obstacles are the plan of God – He is good and all that He does is good, and He is at work in His people.

The truth is that we understand God's power best in the middle of the trying and difficult situations of life.

We appreciate His power even more when we experience the despair first.

Our faith and trust are strengthened when we witness His divine power at work in the impossible situations of our lives.

When I was a kid, we used to sing a song in Sunday School that went like this...

> *Twelve men went to spy in Canaan,*
> *Ten were bad and two were good.*

As an adult I want to disagree. Yes, I understand the sentiment behind that phrase, but the ten weren't bad – they were forgetful. They forgot who was the One who had assumed the responsibility for fulfilling the promise of conquering the land. They believed that they were responsible and if that were the case then they were truly in an impossible situation.

In the middle of the impossible situations, we must believe that nothing is impossible with God!

God will always accomplish what He says He will do; the question is, will we be present when He accomplishes it, or will we have disqualified ourselves?

God is able! He is powerful and mighty no matter what the situation looks like in your life. If He gives you a word of what He is going to do, then nothing can stand in His way. Live in the greater blessing by believing unswervingly in His Word and don't try to do it on your own.

What promise has God spoken to you that seems so impossible right now that you are contemplating turning around and going back?

Who will you choose to be today – one of the ten or one of the two? What will you need to do differently to live in faith that His power is sufficient?

No word from God is without the inherent power to accomplish it!

Chapter 11

A Revelation of His Mercy

Jeremiah 33:2–3 (NIV) [2] *"This is what the LORD says, he who made the earth, the LORD who formed it and established it—the LORD is his name:* [3] *'Call to me and I will answer you and tell you great and unsearchable things you do not know.'*

Mark 1:40–42 (NIV) [40] *A man with leprosy came to him and begged him on his knees, "If you are willing, you can make me clean."* [41] *Filled with compassion, Jesus reached out his hand and touched the man. "I am willing," he said. "Be clean!"* [42] *Immediately the leprosy left him and he was cured.*

Have you ever been so desperate for a change in your situation that you would do just about anything? This was the case of the man with leprosy. His disease had left him physically disfigured.

Leprosy would destroy the skin, and in some cases cause fingers, toes and even the nose to fall off. The disease would have also left him socially despised. There were so many questions and fears surrounding leprosy that the best solution people had was to cast out the lepers from society.

Lepers were required to live in colonies far away from everyone else and if they came to town, they had to cover up completely and ring a bell while shouting unclean as they walked through the town.

Lepers were dead men walking. They had lost it all: family, friends, future. All hope was gone as there was no cure for this disease. I don't know about you, but if that were me, I would be desperate for a change in my situation.

Desperate people do desperate things, so this leper decides to come and ask Jesus to heal him. He comes humbly to Jesus – all his pride was gone. Desperation does that to us.

He braves the people who will tell him to get out of there.

He braves the mad-dog stares he will get for venturing into the world of healthy people, and he comes and falls on his knees. "Jesus, I believe that if you want to, you have the power to heal me."

I love Jesus' response, because it reveals His heart for us. **Filled with compassion.**

Jesus has mercy on him. The theological definition of God's mercy is His goodness toward those in misery and distress.[3] In the leper's distress and misery Jesus responds, not just by feeling sorry for Him, but by doing something about it. Jesus reaches out and touches this man that everyone else was running from and tells Him, "Not only am I feeling sorry for you, but I am also going to do something about it AND I have the power to do what no one else can do – be healed!"

One of my favorite and most treasured stories is of my daughter Allison and her friend Grace praying for a woman with leprosy. They were on a mission trip to India and were visiting a leper colony. Yes, they still exist today!

"God is compassionate, willing AND able."

Their team leader, Justin, had drilled into their heads, "While we pray for physical healing for everyone, not everyone will be healed, but everyone will experience the love of Jesus through us." I love that!

So, there they are, praying for people in the leper colony and not just at a distance, but holding their hands, hugging on them, loving then with human touch. The woman that Allison and Grace were praying for had lost her fingers as a result of the leprosy, they had fallen off and only her thumb remained. While they were praying for the woman, Allison says she felt this strange sensation in her hand – the hand that was holding the leprous woman's hand. When Allison and Grace were done praying, the woman held up her hand to show them and where previously she only had nubs there were fingers fully grown back! Woohoo!! The love and power of God at work even today!

---

[3] Grudem, W. A. (2004). **Systematic theology: an introduction to biblical doctrine** (p. 200). Leicester, England; Grand Rapids, MI: Inter-Varsity Press; Zondervan Pub. House.

God is compassionate, willing, and able!

> ***Ephesians 3:16–20 (TPT)*** *[16] ...I pray that he (God) would unveil within you the unlimited riches of his glory and favor until supernatural strength floods your innermost being with his divine might and explosive power. [17] Then, by constantly using your faith, the life of Christ will be released deep inside you, and the resting place of his love will become the very source and root of your life. [18] Then you will be empowered to discover what every holy one experiences—the great magnitude of the astonishing love of Christ in all its dimensions. How deeply intimate and far-reaching is his love! How enduring and inclusive it is! Endless love beyond measurement that transcends our understanding—this extravagant love pours into you until you are filled to overflowing with the fullness of God! [20] Never doubt God's mighty power to work in you and accomplish all this. He will achieve infinitely more than your greatest request, your most unbelievable dream, and exceed your wildest imagination! He will outdo them all, for his miraculous power constantly energizes you.*

God is willing and able to do more than you could ask or think.

Where do you need to see God's power at work in your life?

What are your next steps to draw near to Him so that you can experience His grace, compassion, and power?

How can you live out the heart of God to be compassionate towards others?

Chapter 12

A Revelation of His Love

God is love

The dictionary's definition of love is *"an intense feeling of deep affection."* To be honest, I consider it an incomplete definition. I would propose that a better definition of love is...

"An intense feeling of deep affection that moves us to give of ourselves, no matter the cost, in order to bring about good for the recipient of those feelings of affection."

My amazing dad would constantly remind us kids that love is an action word. It is more than a feeling or concept – it is passion that generates action.

The Bible tells us that <u>God is the standard of love</u> – He is love.

> ***1 John 4:8 (NIV)*** *[8] Whoever does not love does not know God, because God is love.*

For there to be love there must be an object of affection and throughout the Bible we see God's love displayed.

The Father loves the Son.
> **John 3:35 (NIV)** [35] *The Father loves the Son and has placed everything in his hands.*

The Son loves the Father.
> **John 14:31 (TPT)** [31] *I am doing exactly what the Father destined for me to accomplish, so that the world will discover how much I love my Father..."*

God loves the people of the world.
> **1 John 4:10 (NIV)** [10] *This is love: not that we loved God, but that he loved us and sent his Son as an atoning sacrifice for our sins.*

> **Romans 5:8 (The Message)** [8] *But God put his love on the line for us by offering his Son in sacrificial death while we were of no use whatever to him.*

> **John 3:16 (The Message)** [16] *"This is how much God loved the world: He gave his Son, his one and only Son. And this is why: so that no one need be destroyed; by believing in him, anyone can have a whole and lasting life.*

Looking at all those verses on love (starting with John 3:35), what are some of the characteristics of God's love that we see? Did you notice that every characteristic of love that you would mention carries the action of God giving of Himself to us in order to bring us life, joy, freedom and provision? This is God's nature – He just can't help Himself!

God is love and He loves us. Let that sink in for a moment.

I love the picture that David paints of that realization that he is loved by God. Eugene Peterson does such an awesome job of describing it…

> **Psalm 18:16–19 (The Message)** [16] *But me he caught—reached all the way from sky to sea; he pulled me out of that ocean of hate,* [17] *that enemy chaos, the void in which I was drowning.* [18] *They hit me when I was down, but GOD stuck by me.* [19] *He stood me up on a wide-open field; I stood there saved—surprised to be loved!*

(I encourage you to read the whole Psalm in *The Message*)

The very standard of love has placed His affections on us. He loves me so I can expect that He will freely, willingly, and generously give of Himself to bring about what is best for me. He loves me freely and willingly which means that His love is not earned or deserved. We have been programmed to believe that love is conditional – if you do this then I will accept and love you – but God says,

"My love for you is unconditional, you don't have to do anything for me to love you."

Mind blowing! I wonder how many of us are laboring under believing that we earn God's love by jumping through a bunch of hoops and regulations so that He will somehow feel more affection towards us than He already has.

We could stop there and that would be an amazing thing – but let's go for Greater! Revelation leads to invitation and an opportunity to trust and obey. Now that we have a revelation of God's love we are invited to love as He loves: to love Him as He loves us, and to love others as He loves them. Ouch! Can't we just stop with He loves me?

How do we love God?

As we have seen God demonstrate, love is doing what is best for another regardless of the cost, so if we love God then we should be reciprocating that action. We imitate Him.

God's love is demonstrated in that He gave Himself freely for what would bring us true joy, so we can love God by giving ourselves to what brings joy to God. Which begs the question: What brings God joy?

> *1 John 5:3 (NIV)* [3] *This is love for God: to obey his commands. And his commands are not burdensome,*

> *1 John 2:15 (CEV)* [15] *Don't love the world or anything that belongs to the world. If you love the world, you cannot love the Father.*

Remember that motivation is important – there is an order. Actions follow affection. I obey God's commands because I love Him and want to give myself to what brings Him joy. I don't obey His commands to earn His love. I obey His commands to bring Him joy because I love Him. Stop and think about that carefully because it changes everything.

"God stuck by me. He stood me up on a wide-open field; I stood there saved – surprised to be loved!"

How have you experienced the love of God?

What does loving God look like for you?

Ask the Holy Spirit to show you areas of your life where you can love God more fully.

Ephesians 3:17–19 (NIV) [17] *... I pray that you, being rooted and established in love,* [18] *may have power, together with all the saints, to grasp how wide and long and high and deep is the love of Christ,* [19] *and to know this love that surpasses knowledge—that you may be filled to the measure of all the fullness of God.*

The universal expectation of what every child of God should experience is the amazing and multi-dimensional love of God

- How far reaching it is
- How intimate it is
- How enduring it is
- How inclusive it is
- How incomprehensible it is
- How extravagant it is

Write down times when you have experienced each of these facets of the love of God.

Chapter 13

A Revelation of His Heart

The revelation of God's love is an invitation to love as He loves.

To love God is to do what brings Him joy no matter the cost to us. Loving Him means obeying His commands and loving Him over the things of this world. But there is something else that brings God joy that we should do to love Him – we are to love people. We are to give of ourselves, no matter the cost, to bring about good for the people that God loves.

God Loves People

Many years ago, I read a modern-day parable that sought to explain the love God has for people, I weep every time I read it because it reminds me of the depth of love the Father God has for me.

There was once a bridge that spanned a large river. During most of the day the bridge sat with its length running up and down the river paralleled with the banks, allowing ships to pass through freely on both sides of the bridge. But at certain times each day, a train would come along, and the bridge would be turned sideways across the river, allowing the train to cross it.

A switchman sat in a shack on one side of the river where he operated the controls to turn the bridge and lock it into place as the train crossed.

One evening as the switchman was waiting for the last train of the day to come, he looked off into the distance through the dimming twilight and caught sight of the train lights. He stepped onto the control and waited until the train was within a prescribed distance. Then he was to turn the bridge. He turned the bridge into position, but, to his horror, he found the locking control did not work. If the bridge was not securely in position, it would cause the train to jump the track and go crashing into the river. This would be a passenger train with MANY people aboard.

He left the bridge turned across the river and hurried across the bridge to the other side of the river, where there was a lever switch he could hold to operate the lock manually.

He would have to hold the lever back firmly as the train crossed. He could hear the rumble of the train now, and he took hold of the lever and leaned backward to apply his weight to it, locking the bridge. He kept applying the pressure to keep the mechanism locked. Many lives depended on this man's strength.

Then, coming across the bridge from the direction of his control shack, he heard a sound that made his blood run cold.

"Daddy, where are you?" His four-year-old son was crossing the bridge to look for him. His first impulse was to cry out to the child, "Run! Run!" But the train was too close; the tiny legs would never make it across the bridge in time.

The man almost left his lever to snatch up his son and carry him to safety. But he realized that he could not get back to the lever in time if he saved his son.

Either many people on the train or his own son – must die.

> *"Love is doing what is best for another no matter with it costs you."*

He took but a moment to make his decision. The train sped safely and swiftly on its way, and no one aboard was even aware of the tiny broken body thrown mercilessly into the river by the on-rushing train.[4]

> *John 3:16 (The Message)* [16] *"This is how much God loved the world: He gave his Son, his one and only Son. And this is why: so that no one need be destroyed; by believing in him, anyone can have a whole and lasting life.*

> *1 John 4:10 (NIV)* [10] *This is love: not that we loved God, but that he loved us and sent his Son as an atoning sacrifice for our sins.*

> *Romans 5:8 (The Message)* [8] *But God put his love on the line for us by offering his Son in sacrificial death while we were of no use whatever to him.*

---

[4] **To Sacrifice a Son: An Allegory** by Dennis E Hensley

God loves people.

It brings Him joy when we love others as He loves.

> **John 15:12–13 (NIV)** [12] *My command is this: Love each other as I have loved you.* [13] *Greater love has no one than this, that he lay down his life for his friends.*

How then should we love people?

> **Matthew 9:35–38 (TPT)** [35] *Jesus walked throughout the region with the joyful message of God's kingdom realm. He taught in their meeting houses, and wherever he went he demonstrated God's power by healing every kind of disease and illness.* [36] *When he saw the vast crowds of people, Jesus' heart was deeply moved with compassion, because they seemed weary and helpless, like wandering sheep without a shepherd.* [37] *He turned to his disciples and said, "The harvest is huge and ripe! But there are not enough harvesters to bring it all in.* [38] *As you go, plead with the Owner of the Harvest to thrust out many more reapers to harvest his grain!"*

From this passage Jesus shows us what loving others look like.

- He goes and meets people where they are and does not wait for them to come to Him.
- He shares the Good News that the Father loves them and desires relationship with them.
- He does everything in His power to heal and help them in their misery.
- He is compassionate towards them – empathetic and kind.
- He recruits others to help people.

There are so many other ways we are to love people but let me mention one more that is one of the biggest ways. We love by forgiving people of things they may have done to hurt or offend us. That is a tough one, isn't it?

Take a moment to read the following passage and allow the Holy Spirit to speak to you about loving God by loving others.

> *1 Corinthians 13:4–7 (The Message)* [4] *Love never gives up. Love cares more for others than for self. Love doesn't want what it doesn't have. Love doesn't strut, Doesn't have a swelled head,* [5] *Doesn't force itself on others, Isn't always "me first," Doesn't fly off the handle, Doesn't keep score of the sins of others,* [6] *Doesn't revel when others grovel, Takes pleasure in the flowering of truth,* [7] *Puts up with anything, Trusts God always, Always looks for the best, Never looks back, But keeps going to the end.*

How are you doing loving God by loving people?

Who is God asking you to love more deeply?
What would that practically look like? Remember, love is doing what's best for another no matter what it costs you.
Who do you need to forgive? How will you practically walk that out?

Chapter 14

Revelation

If you are reading this as a devotional, then take today and spend some time reviewing what we have been reading and ruminating on in the last six chapters. Meditate on a characteristic of God and allow Him to show you a greater revelation of Himself.

Go to a place where you can have uninterrupted time. Go sit in the park, take a long and leisurely walk, wake up early before everyone else and sit in the living room alone...

Ask God to speak to you.

Father what is on Your heart?

How would you like me to pray?

For whom do you want me to pray?

Then spend time listening and responding.

Write down anything you feel that God is speaking to you. If it requires action on your part, then what is your next step?

Use ACTS to pray.
- Adoration
- Confession
- Thanksgiving
- Supplication – my prayer requests.

Whatever you do, the goal is to draw near to God. To seek Him, to allow Him to reveal Himself to you, to give Him unhindered and unhurried time.

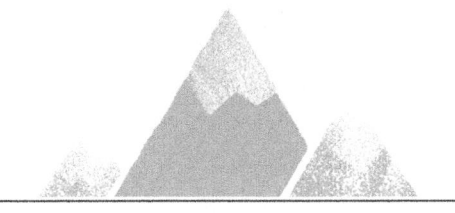

greater increase
(blessings, abundance)

Invitation followed by obedience leads to intimacy.
Intimacy leads to revelation.
Revelation leads to greater invitation.

Chapter 15

Ask For It

Intimacy gives us audience to discover the heart of God. We discover his goodness and love for us and others. Intimacy now gives us audience to petition God.

In Exodus 32 and 33 we drop in on Moses and the Israelites just after they had come out of Egypt and on their way to the promised land. Moses had been gone for a few weeks, up on Mount Sinai where God had been instructing him on how the Israelites were to live and worship. He comes down from the mountain to a sight that made his blood boil. The people were in a frenzy, worshipping a golden calf that they had built.

As an aside, one of the funniest things I have ever read in the Bible was in this story.

> ***Exodus 32:21–24 (NIV)*** *[21] He said to Aaron, "What did these people do to you, that you led them into such great sin?" [22] "Do not be angry, my lord," Aaron answered. "You know how prone*

> *these people are to evil. [23] They said to me, 'Make*
> *us gods who will go before us. As for this fellow*
> *Moses who brought us up out of Egypt, we don't*
> *know what has happened to him.' [24] So I told*
> *them, 'Whoever has any gold jewelry, take it off.'*
> *Then they gave me the gold, and I threw it into*
> *the fire, and out came this calf!"*

Moses glares at his brother Aaron and asked, "What have you done and what in the world were you thinking?"

"Ummm, yeah Mo, I threw in the gold and ummm…this calf thing just came out!"

LOL!! I love the Contemporary English Bible's version of Aaron's answer…

> **Exodus 32:24 (CEV)** [24] *Then I asked them to bring*
> *me their gold earrings. They took them off and*
> *gave them to me. I threw the gold into a fire, and*
> *out came this bull.*

Sounds like a lot of bull came out of that fire! Anyway, back to our story.

In a few short weeks, the people of God had put aside their honor and reverence for Him and taken up the ways of the cultures around them. Moses was appalled and embarrassed, and God was angry. God's anger burned against the Israelites so much so that He vowed that He would destroy them, but Moses pleaded with God on their behalf and God decided not to destroy them.

Instead, God decided that He would simply wash His hands of them. He told Moses that He would keep His word about giving them the land that He had promised Abraham, but from here on out He was not going to be with them. Honestly, I am not sure which is worse, being struck down by God or being without His presence in my everyday living.

Moses felt that being without God's presence was too harsh a punishment so again he goes back to God and pleads on behalf of the people. Remember he has already pleaded before God to not destroy them and now he is asking for more.

> **Exodus 33:7–11 (NIV)** [7] *Now Moses used to take a tent and pitch it outside the camp some distance away, calling it the "tent of meeting." Anyone inquiring of the LORD would go to the tent of meeting outside the camp.* [8] *And whenever Moses went out to the tent, all the people rose and stood at the entrances to their tents, watching Moses until he entered the tent...*[11] *The LORD would speak to Moses face to face, as a man speaks with his friend.*

> **Exodus 33:12–19 (NIV)** [12] *Moses said to the LORD, "You have been telling me, 'Lead these people, but you have not let me know whom you will send with me. You have said, 'I know you by name and you have found favor with me.'* [13] *If you are pleased with me, teach me your ways so I may know you and continue to find favor with you. Remember that this nation is your people."* [14] *The LORD replied, "My Presence will go with you, and I will give you rest."* [15] *Then Moses said to him, "If your Presence does not go with us, do not send us up from here.* [16] *How will anyone know that you are pleased with me and with your people unless you go with us? What else will distinguish me and your people from all the other people on the face of the earth?"* [17] *And the LORD said to Moses, "I will do the very thing you have asked, because I*

am pleased with you and I know you by name." [18]
Then Moses said, "Now show me your glory." [19]
And the LORD said, "I will cause all my goodness to
pass in front of you, and I will proclaim my name,
the LORD, in your presence. I will have mercy on
whom I will have mercy, and I will have
compassion on whom I will have compassion.

You see the principle in action?
Invitation followed by obedience leads to intimacy.
Intimacy leads to revelation.

God invites Moses to follow Him and lead the people out of slavery. Moses obeys and the obedience leads Moses to walk in deeper relationship with God. In the relationship God reveals Himself to Moses. The revelation led to a greater invitation – God speaking to Moses as a friend – and greater invitation, coupled with obedience, led to greater intimacy. It is because of that greater intimacy that Moses is able to plead for a nation.

"God thank you for not destroying these people, but I need more than that – I need your presence to go with us. You see if You are not with us then we are as good as dead anyway."

"Moses could ask for Greater because of
intimacy."

You see the same thing with David.

God invites David to be in relationship with Him and David obeys and pursues God. He longs for His presence. "As the deer pants for the water, so my soul longs after you," he declared. The result is that God gives David a promise. Ask me for what you want.

> ***Psalm 2:7–8 (CEV)*** *[7] I will tell the promise that the LORD made to me: "You are my son, because today I have become your father. [8] Ask me for the nations, and every nation on earth will belong to you.*

What is it that you desire greater increase and blessing in? For David, as the ruler of a nation, he desired the ruling of nations so God said, "You are the ruler of a nation, but ask me for the nations and I will give them to you!"

For Moses it was the lives of the people, and the ongoing presence of God, and God gave it. And did you notice that God gave Moses greater revelation? Look at Exodus 33:18-19 again. God promised to not remove His presence from the nation and to Moses He gave a greater revelation of Himself to him because he asked for it! Go for Greater!

What is it that you desire greater increase and blessing in?

Where is God inviting you to come and join Him and you are hesitating to obey?

Are you drawing near to God in intimacy? What is keeping you from it?

Where do you need to ask God for more?

Chapter 16

Ask For It Again

There is a principle to experiencing Greater that I am uncomfortable with – it is the idea of persistence. If I am honest, I struggle with not wanting to be a nuisance to God. I don't want to impose on His goodness. Over the years I have come to rely on some principles from His Word that encourage me to go for it. Here are a few…

Be bold
Time after time in the Bible you see that God answers those who are not afraid to ask. God says, "Call to me and I will answer you." (Jeremiah 33:3)

In the New Testament you see time and again people asking Jesus to heal them, and He responded. The blind man. The leper. But probably one of my favorites is the woman with the issue of blood.

> *Mark 5:25–34 (NIV) 25 And a woman was there who had been subject to bleeding for twelve years. 26 She had suffered a great deal under the*

*care of many doctors and had spent all she had,
yet instead of getting better she grew worse. ²⁷*
*When she heard about Jesus, she came up behind
him in the crowd and touched his cloak, ²⁸*
*because she thought, "If I just touch his clothes, I
will be healed." ²⁹ Immediately her bleeding
stopped and she felt in her body that she was
freed from her suffering. ³⁰ At once Jesus realized
that power had gone out from him. He turned
around in the crowd and asked, "Who touched
my clothes?" ³¹ "You see the people crowding
against you," his disciples answered, "and yet you
can ask, 'Who touched me?'" ³² But Jesus kept
looking around to see who had done it. ³³ Then
the woman, knowing what had happened to her,
came and fell at his feet and, trembling with fear,
told him the whole truth. ³⁴ He said to her,
"Daughter, your faith has healed you. Go in peace
and be freed from your suffering."*

Some would say she was presumptuous, not me, I love her boldness, it inspires me to be bold. It is that boldness that brings her into the Greater.

Be persistent
Jesus tells us that when we ask, we should keep on asking. (Matt 7:7) On a number of occasions Jesus chided the disciples for their lack of faith and I often wondered what He meant.

*Matthew 17:14–20 (NIV) ¹⁴ When they came to
the crowd, a man approached Jesus and knelt
before him. ¹⁵ "Lord, have mercy on my son," he
said. "He has seizures and is suffering greatly. He*

often falls into the fire or into the water. [16] I brought him to your disciples, but they could not heal him." [17] "O unbelieving and perverse generation," Jesus replied, "how long shall I stay with you? How long shall I put up with you? Bring the boy here to me." [18] Jesus rebuked the demon, and it came out of the boy, and he was healed from that moment. [19] Then the disciples came to Jesus in private and asked, "Why couldn't we drive it out?" [20] He replied, "Because you have so little faith. I tell you the truth, if you have faith as small as a mustard seed, you can say to this mountain, 'Move from here to there' and it will move. Nothing will be impossible for you."

I know what you may be thinking, "I am confused – God says we need only have the faith the size of a mustard seed to do the impossible. A mustard seed size faith. Such a small amount. So how come they were not able to drive out the demon?"

What Jesus is saying is that we all have the faith within us to obey him. The smallest amount of faith can bring about the impossible, but the amount of faith we have in us is not the issue here - what we are lacking is the persistent application of that mustard seed.

We give up too soon! We see the circumstances and we start to second guess the word of God. We stop believing in the power of God to accomplish what He has called us to, and we panic and fear causes us to stop applying the faith seed.

Keep on asking, keep on knocking. In Luke 18:1-8 Jesus tells the parable of a persistent widow, and He ends by saying this…

Luke 18:7–8 (TPT) [7] *"Don't you know that God,
the true judge, will grant justice to all of his
chosen ones who cry out to him night and day?
He will pour out his Spirit upon them. He will not
delay to answer you and give you what you ask
for.* [8] *God will give swift justice to those who don't
give up. So be ever praying, ever expecting, just
like the widow was with the judge..."*

Remember His nature

Sometimes we are uncomfortable being persistent in asking God for greater because we forget who He is. Our understanding of who He is will lead to greater boldness to ask again and again. Allow me to remind you of who He is...

He is good – His intentions towards us are never evil. He wants to pour out His favor and blessings on us and how He feels about us is never swayed by what we do – He loves us no matter what!

He is powerful – God has the ability to do whatever He wills. There is nothing too difficult for Him to accomplish.

---
*"Sometimes we are uncomfortable being
persistent in asking God for greater because we
forget who He is."*

He is willing – sometimes we believe that He is powerful, but we think that He is not willing to work on our behalf. Nothing is further from the truth. God is able and willing to answer our prayers.

He loves you – Don't you forget it! He loves you and wants to pour out His favor upon you. He wants to give you Greater!

So go for it! Ask for more. Ask and keep on asking! Don't feel ashamed! And most of all trust that in His love and goodness He knows what is best for you and wants to give it to you!

What are some things that you have stopped asking God for that you need to keep on asking and seeking Him for?

If your motivation is for His glory, then be bold and keep on asking.

Chapter 17

Greater Peace

Mark 4:35–40 (NIV) [35] *That day when evening came, he said to his disciples, "Let us go over to the other side."* [36] *Leaving the crowd behind, they took him along, just as he was, in the boat. There were also other boats with him.* [37] *A furious squall came up, and the waves broke over the boat, so that it was nearly swamped.* [38] *Jesus was in the stern, sleeping on a cushion. The disciples woke him and said to him, "Teacher, don't you care if we drown?"* [39] *He got up, rebuked the wind and said to the waves, "Quiet! Be still!" Then the wind died down and it was completely calm.* [40] *He said to his disciples, "Why are you so afraid? Do you still have no faith?"*

"He said to his disciples..."

No word from God is without the inherent power to accomplish it! If God said it then He will accomplish it. The journey over to the other side was obedience to a direct word from God. Jesus was the one who said to them, "Let's go over to the other side."

"A furious squall came up"

So here we are going along, and we have decided to follow Jesus, no turning back, no turning back. And things are hunky dunky. Life is good and there is smooth sailing. You have given it all up to follow Jesus and you think that with Jesus in the boat nothing can go wrong. Right? Wrong!

Where have we gotten this notion that the presence of God means the absence of trouble? Not from the Bible. Everywhere you look God was with His people, but they experienced hardships and trials, pain, and suffering. Paul says I have been pressed by the cares of this life, crushed by situations. Persecuted, beaten, left for dead. During all these things God was always with Paul.

Some of us even have the notion that if we are experiencing hardships then it must be because we did something wrong. Jesus tells us that this is not always the case...

> **John 16:33 (NIV)** *33 "I have told you these things, so that in me you may have peace. In this world you will have trouble. But take heart! I have overcome the world."*

Some mistakenly believe that hardships mean that God has abandoned them – but where was Jesus? He was in the boat with them.

From out of nowhere there comes this furious storm. One minute life is all fine, you are following Jesus, and everything is amazing and now suddenly you find yourself in the middle of a storm fighting for your life.

The boss calls you in and tells you that you have been laid off. This is all you know how to do and there are no companies around that would hire you because all the positions are filled. And the storm begins to blow.

You have been healthy all your life and now out of nowhere everything begins to shut down and your health begins to fail. And the winds begin to kick up.

Your spouse says, "I have been living a lie. The truth is I don't love you anymore, I'm leaving, I want a divorce." And the waves begin to rise.

The IRS calls and tell you that there has been a discrepancy on your taxes and now you owe $20,000 and you can't even afford to buy a gallon of milk for the kids much less think about that much money. The water begins to swamp the boat.

And your first reaction is fear.
Spine chilling, motion paralyzing fear.
You know beyond a shadow of a doubt that your life is over and what makes it even worse is it seems that Jesus is asleep and doesn't even care about your situation. He is just going to let you drown. You begin to think. "If I had stayed on the shore none of this would have happened. I would still have my possessions and peace of mind."

Christian Philosopher, Francis Schaeffer, said,

"...the greatest threat to the cause of Christ...would be if the United States became a nation filled with Christians whose goal in life is personal safety, peace and prosperity...and sadly more people turn around and head for the shore back to so-called safety the moment the storm clouds roll in and they never fulfill the plan of God for their lives. When we do that what happens is that our borders shrink, our boundaries get smaller, and we get farther and farther away from God – not farther away from risk or storms. We fence ourselves off with a false sense of security and tie ourselves to a stake that keeps us from everything including God. Our love for Him will grow cold, our passion damp. After all, why do we need him if we have everything buttoned down tight in our own little world." [5]

What a sad way to live.

Recently the Holy Spirit led me back to Psalm 23.

Psalm 23:5 (NIV) [5] *You prepare a table before me in the presence of my enemies.*

I am captivated by the picture that we are seated in the presence of Jesus feasting at His table. How awesome is that? Here is the problem though, most of us are more focused on the second part of the verse: the presence of my enemies. You have no peace because all you can see is the enemy.

"We are seated in the presence of Jesus yet all we tend to focus on is the enemy in the room."

Here you are sitting in the presence of Jesus, with a feast available for you and all you can see is the enemy in the room. You are so focused on the enemy you can't see that

---

[5] **The Church At The End of the 20th Century** Francis Shaeffer January 1971

you are winning. Here it is you are seated in His presence, surrounded by a feast. But you are looking at the wind and the waves. You are looking at the enemy in the room.

You know why Jesus kept the enemy in the room? He wants you to know that the enemy has no power over you. His stinger has been removed. He is defeated. He is making the devil watch you feast.

The winds and the waves are nothing to worry about because we can trust in the word of God. The wind and the waves will come and go. The devil will always be sitting in the room. Life will always have hardships, trials, pain, and suffering. But more importantly Jesus is with us, and He is offering us a feast. Will you be fearful, or will you feast in His presence?

Experience greater peace by trusting in the word of God that has the power to accomplish what He has declared over you, in you and about you!

> ***Isaiah 41:10 (NIV)*** *So do not fear, for I am with you; do not be dismayed, for I am your God. I will strengthen you and help you; I will uphold you with my righteous right hand.*

> ***Isaiah 26:3–4 (CEV)*** *[3] The LORD gives perfect peace to those whose faith is firm. [4] So always trust the LORD because he is forever our mighty rock.*

What situations are you facing where you are responding in fear?

What does God's Word say about your circumstances and situations? Look for those promises for they are the basis of our faith. If you don't know what God's Word says, talk to someone who can help you.

Focus on the feast God has set before you and not on the presence of the enemy. Take a moment to recall God's blessings in your life. It may be tough at first because it takes a moment to get out of fear mode but stick with it and start feasting.

Chapter 18

Greater Joy

Psalm 16:11 (NKJV) [11] *You will show me the path of life; In Your presence is fullness of joy; At Your right hand are pleasures forevermore.*

Most people don't enjoy life; they just endure it.
We think that life must be perfect for us to be happy.
If I could just change my situation, life would be great.
If I could just get rid of all my problems...

But there's no such thing as a problem free life.

If you're going to learn to be joyful, you must learn to be joyful in the situation, in the problems, in the very experiences of life.

"Happiness" comes from the word "happenstance" from which we get the word "circumstance".
It depends on happenings. But joy...well, that is internal.

Happiness is external. You have a happy time at Disneyland, you leave, and you lose your happiness.

Joy is greater.

> **Philippians 1:12-26 (NIV)** [12]*Now I want you to know, brothers, that what has happened to me has really served to advance the gospel.* [13]*As a result, it has become clear throughout the whole palace guard and to everyone else that I am in chains for Christ.* [14]*Because of my chains, most of the brothers in the Lord have been encouraged to speak the word of God more courageously and fearlessly.* [15]*It is true that some preach Christ out of envy and rivalry, but others out of goodwill.* [16]*The latter do so in love, knowing that I am put here for the defense of the gospel.* [17]*The former preach Christ out of selfish ambition, not sincerely, supposing that they can stir up trouble for me while I am in chains.* [18]*But what does it matter? The important thing is that in every way, whether from false motives or true, Christ is preached. And because of this I rejoice. Yes, and I will continue to rejoice,* [19]*for I know that through your prayers and the help given by the Spirit of Jesus Christ, what has happened to me will turn out for my deliverance.* [20]*I eagerly expect and hope that I will in no way be ashamed, but will have sufficient courage so that now as always Christ will be exalted in my body, whether by life or by death.* [21]*For to me, to live is Christ and to die is gain.* [22]*If I am to go on living in the body, this will mean fruitful labor for me. Yet what shall I choose? I do not know!* [23]*I am torn between the*

two: I desire to depart and be with Christ, which is better by far; [24]but it is more necessary for you that I remain in the body. [25]Convinced of this, I know that I will remain, and I will continue with all of you for your progress and joy in the faith, [26]so that through my being with you again your joy in Christ Jesus will overflow on account of me.

The background of the story today is that Paul, for the last four years, has been in miserable circumstances.

He's spent two years in prison in Caesarea for a trumped-up charge.

Then he's put on a ship to go to Rome to appear before Nero who is not known for his niceties towards Christians.

On the way he's shipwrecked, stranded on an island, bitten by a poisonous snake, waits the winter there, continues to Rome, and spends another two years in prison awaiting trial to be executed.

During this two-year period in Rome, he is chained to a guard for 24 hours a day.

He has absolutely no privacy. Every six hours he gets a new guard.

Yet despite all of these situations, Paul says in...
> **Phil. 1:18 (TLB)** *"I rejoice and I will continue to rejoice."*

What's Paul's secret? How does he...
- stay positive in prison,
- triumph over troubles,
- delight in difficulties,
- stay so happy, positive, joyful although everything has not turned out the way he planned it?

Paul gives us his secret.

You want greater joy? Have the right perspective!

Everyone has problems!

Your problems are not so important as how you are looking at those problems. The way you look at that problem is much more important than the problem. Your perspective makes the difference.

v. 12 "Now I want you to know, brothers, that what has happened to me has really served to advance the gospel."

I can see the best even in the worst. I can see God at work in the problems even when they don't go my way.

Non-believers are being witnessed to in my attitude toward them, believers are being encouraged.

"Change your perspective!"

v. 13: "As a result it has become clear throughout the whole palace guard and to everyone else that I am in chains for Christ."

Paul had always wanted to go to Rome. He meant to have a crusade. Instead, God put him in prison where he would write the New Testament.

He's chained to the palace guard. The praetorium guard were the elite troops of the Roman Empire, personally chosen by Caesar to be his bodyguards. They were the highest paid people of the empire. When they retired after 12 years, they were made leaders in Rome.

There is not a more strategic group that Paul could witness to if he's going to reach the Roman empire.

So, look at this from a different perspective…

God puts Paul in Rome. Nero pays the bill and chains a future leader of Rome to him every six hours.

In two years at six-hour shifts, Paul would have witnessed to 2,290 guards, if there were never repeat guards.

These guards had an inside route to the emperor and as a result even some of Nero's family became believers. History tells us that Nero had his wife, mother and children killed because they became believers. A "chain" reaction. Paul had a captive audience.

v. 14 "Because of my chains most of the brothers in the Lord have been encouraged to speak the word of God more courageously and fearlessly."

Paul's perspective – *"My attitude towards problems has encouraged other people."* Courage is contagious. It spreads like wildfire. Other believers became bold because of Paul being bold.

If you are going to have joy in your life, this is the perspective you need to live from…

> **Romans 8:28 (TLB)** *[28]And we know that ALL that happens to us is working for our good if we love God and are fitting into his plans.*

If you want greater joy, you must constantly remind yourself that God has a purpose behind every one of your problems. When you get this perspective, you are on the way to experiencing Greater. God is at work. He loves you and has a plan and destiny for you, and it is always good. Oh joy!

Take some time today to look at your toughest situations and reframe them from a heavenly perspective.

Chapter 19

Greater Freedom

1 Kings 17:1–6 (NIV) ¹ *Now Elijah the Tishbite, from Tishbe in Gilead, said to Ahab, "As the LORD, the God of Israel, lives, whom I serve, there will be neither dew nor rain in the next few years except at my word." ² Then the word of the LORD came to Elijah: ³ "Leave here, turn eastward and hide in the Kerith Ravine, east of the Jordan. ⁴ You will drink from the brook, and I have ordered the ravens to feed you there." ⁵ So he did what the LORD had told him. He went to the Kerith Ravine, east of the Jordan, and stayed there. ⁶ The ravens brought him bread and meat in the morning and bread and meat in the evening, and he drank from the brook.*

I am guessing that right now that you may be thinking, what does this verse have to do with freedom? I want to look at this idea of greater freedom from a little bit different perspective. I initially thought of titling today, Greater Courage, but I really feel freedom is the better understanding. God wants you to live a life that is free of fear. Fear enslaves you. You make life choices based on fear and it wraps you up in chains that keep you from the free life that God offers. While fear enslaves you, obedience to God brings freedom. There is a great freedom that comes when you choose to trust and obey God and allow Him to take care of you. Let's explore this a bit.

King Ahab was a wicked and ungodly man. Here is how the Bible describes him...

> *1 Kings 16:30–33 (NIV)* ³⁰ *Ahab son of Omri did more evil in the eyes of the LORD than any of those before him. ³¹ He not only considered it trivial to commit the sins of Jeroboam son of Nebat, but he also married Jezebel daughter of Ethbaal king of the Sidonians, and began to serve Baal and worship him. ³² He set up an altar for Baal in the temple of Baal that he built in Samaria. ³³ Ahab also made an Asherah pole and did more to provoke the LORD, the God of Israel, to anger than did all the kings of Israel before him.*

Yikes, that is pretty bad. A guy like this does not put up with people who oppose him, so you can imagine Elijah's apprehension when God must have said to him,

"Go to Ahab and rebuke him and tell him that I am going to send a drought to the land."

"Erm, God You sure you want me to do that? In person, not Zoom? He will kill me! AND TBH I don't want there to be a drought in the land, that means that everyone suffers, including me!"

"Elijah, go and speak my words to that wicked man."
"Well I don't want to God but because you said so I will!"

Elijah is obedient to God and delivers the God's message to the king. As expected, he king does not take it well and seeks to kill Elijah. God then informs Elijah that He has prepared a place for Elijah to stay where he will be safe from the king and where God has arranged for him to be cared for. Notice that God did not give any of those details until after Elijah had done what God had asked him to do – then and only then was the provision revealed. **When we trust and obey God there is great freedom** for us because God is taking care of the details. We just need to put one foot in front of the other.

One of the ways we can more easily obey God is through cultivated relationship. The more time I spend with Him, the more I discover who He is and His love for me and the more I am able to trust and obey Him.

"Freedom is only experienced through obedience."

Psalm 27:1-3 (NLT) [1] *The LORD is my light and my salvation— so why should I be afraid? The LORD is my fortress, protecting me from danger, so why should I tremble?* [2] *When evil people come to devour me, when my enemies and foes attack me, they will stumble and fall.* [3] *Though a mighty army surrounds me, my heart will not be afraid. Even if I am attacked, I will remain confident.*

The Lord is my light, strength, and salvation: in other words, He overcomes the darkness that threatens me. He gives me strength to stand and with Him victory is assured.   If God is my light and strength, and I am assured that He will overcome, then the situations and circumstances around me should not cause me to be fearful.   I can look at the circumstances from heaven's perspective and know that God's plans will succeed and now I can live in great freedom – a freedom from fear and a freedom that brings peace and joy.

David could make this public declaration because of his private practice of seeking to spend time with God in fellowship.   It is the understanding of abiding in Christ.

"He who dwells in the secret place of the most High will abide in the shadow of the almighty."

"If you abide in me and my words abide in you."

Living in greater freedom comes because we take time to be with God.   In David's time when a visitor entered his host's tent the host was personally responsible for his protection and provision.   David is saying that he is placing himself willingly in God's tent so that God will be personally responsible for his safety and protection.   And while he is in the tent of the Lord what is he doing? Abiding. But abiding is not a passive thing.   It is not just sitting there mindlessly staring into space.   While in the tent of the Lord we fellowship with Him.   We talk to Him and listen as He talks to us.

> **Psalm 27:4 (TLB)** *⁴The one thing I want from God, the thing I seek most of all, is the privilege of meditating in his Temple, living in his presence every day of my life, delighting in his incomparable perfections and glory.*

As we abide, we behold the beauty of the Lord. God's beauty is not just how He looks but it is the understanding of the richness of His goodness and favor to His people. We need to meditate on God's goodness and favor towards us. Daily. As we meditate on his mercy and grace as well as His Word, it will strengthen us so that we can face each day. We see life from heaven's perspective and live with a sense of hope and joy, being able to worship God with confidence. This is true freedom!

What are the areas of your life where you are fearful and unwilling to trust and obey God?

Ask the Holy Spirit to reveal to you the things that are holding you back from truly living in full obedience.

Remember that the freedom is only experienced when you obey. God has a plan to protect and provide, but He only reveals it to us when we have taken the steps of obedience.

Chapter 20

Greater Provision

1 Kings 17:7–16 (NIV) *7 Some time later the brook dried up because there had been no rain in the land. 8 Then the word of the LORD came to him: 9 "Go at once to Zarephath of Sidon and stay there. I have commanded a widow in that place to supply you with food." 10 So he went to Zarephath. When he came to the town gate, a widow was there gathering sticks. He called to her and asked, "Would you bring me a little water in a jar so I may have a drink?" 11 As she was going to get it, he called, "And bring me, please, a piece of bread." 12 "As surely as the LORD your God lives," she replied, "I don't have any bread—only a handful of flour in a jar and a little oil in a jug. I am gathering a few sticks to take home and make a meal for myself and my son, that we may eat it—and die." 13 Elijah said to her, "Don't be afraid. Go home and do as you have said. But first make*

> *a small cake of bread for me from what you have*
> *and bring it to me, and then make something for*
> *yourself and your son.* [14] *For this is what the LORD,*
> *the God of Israel, says: 'The jar of flour will not be*
> *used up and the jug of oil will not run dry until the*
> *day the LORD gives rain on the land.' "* [15] *She went*
> *away and did as Elijah had told her. So there was*
> *food every day for Elijah and for the woman and*
> *her family.* [16] *For the jar of flour was not used up*
> *and the jug of oil did not run dry, in keeping with*
> *the word of the LORD spoken by Elijah.*

There is so much in this story that speaks to greater provision. Our last glimpse of Elijah was that he had obeyed God and as a result God has provided for him by having him camp out next to a little brook.

I find it significant that God didn't send Elijah to a place of overwhelming abundance. Elijah did not end up at a roaring river, he ended up at a brook. It was a place where there was provision, but he had to work for the provision. He had to go down to the brook and get the water and probably had to figure out a way to filter it to make it drinkable. God did not just drop the water in his lap. That certainly seemed to have happened with the food but not the water. God provided for Elijah by natural and supernatural means.

And then the brook dried up...

Slowly, day by day, it got less and less. And as it did, I wonder what was Elijah's response?

"What is going on here?! Did I miss God?"

"Is He playing games with me?"

"Maybe I missed what God was saying. Maybe it was not the Kerith Brook, what God actually said was go to Garth

Brook – then all of this would be nothing more than a memory."

"God here I am just being obedient to You, and You provide, but then you take it away. So how is this your greater blessing?"

To Elijah's credit, he didn't panic, he stayed where God had instructed him to be. You get it, right? The brook was not the source of provision. God was and still is the provider, and He can use anything and anyone to provide for us. And God had not forgotten Elijah. When the time was right God instructed him to move.

> *"Sometimes the provision runs out in one area because God wants to move us into position for greater blessing."*

When the brook dried up, God told Elijah to go AT ONCE to Zarepath. Remember it is our obedience that leads us into greater blessing. Elijah obeys.

Here is the interesting thing for me in this story – God says that He has commanded a widow in Zarepath to provide for Elijah. This is interesting because of what happens next. When Elijah gets to Zarepath, he meets the widow gathering sticks and asks her for a drink of water and she is quick to oblige, but as she is walking away, he asks for food as well. The widow hesitates. She turns around and tells him she really does not have enough to feed him. But wait, didn't God say that He had commanded the widow to supply Elijah with food? Now she is hesitating to obey the command of God because she only has enough for her and her son to have one last meal. This is always the test of faith – you see, God is not only working on Elijah's behalf, He has good plans for the widow and her son as well. But for her to experience His good plans, she will need to trust and obey.

She hesitates, but Elijah encourages her to do it anyway. Thankfully she chooses to listen to God and the man of God. By faith, she goes home and did as she has been instructed and something amazing happens – greater provision took place! For the next couple of years, the flour and oil never ran dry. She would have never experienced the greater blessing if she had fearfully succumbed to the initial temptation to ignore the word of God to her.

God's greater blessings always includes more than just us!

Here is another observation from this story, God was bringing greater provision to multiple people at the same time, but each needed to do their part for them to experience the greater provision. Elijah had to obey and go at once to Zarepath. Zarephath was about 100 miles from Kerith, and Elijah was a marked man. Ahab and his wife had put a price on his head, so traveling would be a dangerous proposition, but Elijah didn't allow any of that to deter him from doing what God had called him to do. If he had not obeyed, he would not have experienced the greater provision that God had destined for him. The widow also had to obey – she had to give up her last provisions in order to obtain the greater provision. One last meal or many more meals…by faith. Only after she said yes did she experience it.

Sometimes God asks us to do irrational and seemingly counter-intuitive things. In those moments, we need to trust Him and obey because that is when the door opens to greater provision.

Remember that Greater must have a foundation. You must have something in order to have Greater. Greater provision starts with what you have. When you give obediently of the little you have, then and only then does the real Greater start. If you want more you need to give more, pure and simple. Try it. I have yet to see God fail me in this regard.

Are you where God has directed you or are you trying to provide for yourself? Is the place and direction of your life the result of obedience to God?

What is God asking of you that you are fearful of saying yes to?

Who might you be robbing of a greater provision because you are unwilling to say yes to God?

Chapter 21

Greater Revelation

If you are reading this as a devotional, then take today and spend some time reviewing what we have been reading and ruminating on in the last six readings. Meditate on a characteristic of God and allow Him to show you a greater revelation of Himself.

Go to a place where you can have uninterrupted time. Go sit in the park, take a long and leisurely walk, wake up early before everyone else and sit in the living room alone...

Ask God to speak to you.

Father what is on Your heart?

How would you like me to pray?

For whom do you want me to pray?

Then spend time listening and responding.

Write down anything you feel that God is speaking to you. If it requires action on your part, then what is your next step?

Use ACTS to pray.
- Adoration
- Confession
- Thanksgiving
- Supplication – my prayer requests.

Whatever you do, the goal is to draw near to God. To seek Him, to allow Him to reveal Himself to you, to give Him unhindered and unhurried time.

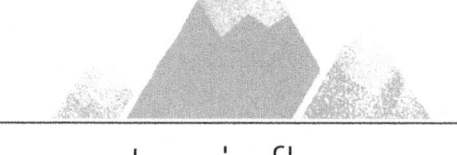

greater influence

Invitation followed by obedience leads to intimacy.
Intimacy leads to revelation.
Revelation leads to greater invitation.

Chapter 22

O Lord Bless Me!

1 Chronicles 4:9–10 (NIV) [9] *Jabez was more honorable than his brothers. His mother had named him Jabez, saying, "I gave birth to him in pain."* [10] *Jabez cried out to the God of Israel, "Oh, that you would bless me and enlarge my territory! Let your hand be with me, and keep me from harm so that I will be free from pain." And God granted his request.*

Doesn't it seem a bit selfish and presumptuous to ask God to bless me and give me greater influence? That was how I felt up until that morning I had the conversation with God about Greater.

It all starts with motivation. It is selfish and self-serving to ask God to bless us just for comfort and convenience. However, when our motivation is to glorify God and fulfill His will here on earth as it is in heaven, then that prayer is exactly what God wants us to pray. If you're yearning for more blessings and greater influence to bring others into the kingdom of heaven, then start praying! Jabez asked God to enlarge all that God had entrusted him with – he asked for Greater because he wanted it to be used to glorify God and accomplish His will on earth as it is in heaven.

So, *what is your motivation for asking God for blessings?* Is it simply for self-gain or it is your desire to use what God has given you to accomplish His will? A good way to measure motivation is to examine how you are utilizing what God has already given you. So many people are waiting for God to bless with great abundance before they will do anything for His glory. The reality is that God is looking to see how we are using the little we have right now for His kingdom purposes.

And how would that prayer look like for you? **Bless me and enlarge my territory.**

Should you be praying for a promotion at work? If your motivation is right, then absolutely.

Should you be asking for greater provision and more resources? Yes, if your motivation is to use it for the glory of God.

Bruce Wilkinson in his book **The Prayer of Jabez** says it this way…

"No matter what your vocation, the highest form of Jabez's prayer for greater might sound something like this…O God and King, please expand my opportunities and my impact in such a way that I touch more lives for Your glory. Let me do more for You!"

Ask God for greater impact and influence.

What is keeping you from asking for Greater? Assuming that your heart is to glorify God and bring about His plan here on earth as it is in heaven, what is keeping you from asking for Greater?

Do you feel that you are unworthy to ask for more?

Do you feel that it is imposing on the generosity of God?

Are you fearful of what will have to be pushed out as God increases in you?

We began this journey together pursuing greater intimacy for a reason.

> *"When we discover who God is we realize that nothing else matters."*

As we come to know God, we realize all those things are minor. The Apostle Paul says it this way...

> **Philippians 3:7–8 (NIV)** [7] *But whatever was to my profit I now consider loss for the sake of Christ.* [8] *What is more, I consider everything a loss compared to the surpassing greatness of knowing Christ Jesus my Lord, for whose sake I have lost all things. I consider them rubbish, that I may gain Christ*

When we discover who God is we realize that nothing else matters. We are not unworthy. We are worthy because He deems us worthy. He believes in us more that we believe in ourselves.

He is not a stingy God – He wants to pour out blessings upon His children. And His blessings are unlimited.

When we discover who God is we know that we have nothing to fear. Everything we "lose" will be returned in greater dimension.

What is keeping you from praying the prayer of Jabez? Why not pray it every day for the next year? Write it out and carry it with you. Put it on the home screen of your phone. Tape it up on the mirror in the bathroom. Every day pray this prayer and here is what I know will happen – God will grant your request!

> ***Matthew 5:13–16 (GW)*** *¹³ "You are salt for the earth. But if salt loses its taste, how will it be made salty again? It is no longer good for anything except to be thrown out and trampled on by people. ¹⁴ "You are light for the world. A city cannot be hidden when it is located on a hill. ¹⁵ No one lights a lamp and puts it under a basket. Instead, everyone who lights a lamp puts it on a lamp stand. Then its light shines on everyone in the house. ¹⁶ In the same way let your light shine in front of people. Then they will see the good that you do and praise your Father in heaven.*

Chapter 23

Promotion

1 Samuel 16:14-23 (MSG) [14] *At that very moment the Spirit of GOD left Saul and in its place a black mood sent by GOD settled on him. He was terrified.* [15] *Saul's advisors said, "This awful tormenting depression from God is making your life miserable.* [16] *O master, let us help. Let us look for someone who can play the harp. When the black mood from God moves in, he'll play his music and you'll feel better."* [17] *Saul told his servants, "Go ahead. Find me someone who can play well and bring him to me."* [18] *One of the young men spoke up, "I know someone. I've seen him myself: the son of Jesse of Bethlehem, an excellent musician. He's also courageous, of age, well-spoken, and good-looking. And GOD is with him."* [19] *So Saul sent messengers to Jesse requesting, "Send your son David to me, the one who tends the sheep."* [20] *Jesse took a donkey, loaded it with a couple of loaves of bread, a flask*

> *of wine, and a young goat, and sent his son David with it to Saul.* [21] *David came to Saul and stood before him. Saul liked him immediately and made him his right-hand man.* [22] *Saul sent word back to Jesse: "Thank you. David will stay here. He's just the one I was looking for. I'm very impressed by him."* [23] *After that, whenever the bad depression from God tormented Saul, David got out his harp and played. That would calm Saul down, and he would feel better as the moodiness lifted.*

A lot of times we pray for greater influence and God does not give it right away – there is a waiting period. That waiting period is really important. it is not a time to sit back and twiddle our thumbs – we are to be active. There is a lot to do in the waiting. Look at David.

Saul's palace is in Gibeah which is 85 miles from Bethlehem. David's hometown is this little village in the back country. My wife grew up in Midwest America in such a small town that there was only one traffic signal. Bethlehem is so small they don't even have a traffic signal! No one in the town thinks that they are going to be in the center of the action, or a bigwig in the palace; no matter how talented they are. But there is more to life than talent - there is God's plans and purposes. God was the one who created David to be strong, handsome, and talented at music, but talent is not enough, David had to develop those talents and develop his character.

A musician can be talented, but he/she must work at the music in order to be skilled. There is a lot of practice that must be done for someone to become skilled at an instrument even if they are a natural at it. More than once the Bible describes David as being skilled on the harp and I believe that a lot of practice was involved for him to stand out from the rest of the harpists that people knew. That is why when the king needed a musician, someone in the palace suggested a little-known kid from a backwoods little town called Bethlehem.

> *"Promotion is not about self-advancement; it is about advancing the plans and purposes of God."*

It is funny how God works it out for the doors to be opened for us. A young man in Saul's court recommended David. What are the chances of that? How does someone who has the king's ear also know about a kid in a no-traffic-signal-town in the middle of nowhere? Coincidence? HA! No way – it was the providential hand of God providing promotion to David. Just as important to this story is the fact that when David was given the opportunity, he was ready and able to make the most of it. He had practiced and he was filled with the Spirit of God and when he began to play God used it to help Saul.

It does not matter where you are - when it is time for promotion, God makes a way for us so that His will and purposes will be fulfilled.

It is your responsibility to hone your talents so that when the time comes, and God places you in positions of influence, you are able to properly use that influence to accomplish God's will.

It is not about your self-advancement; it is about advancing the plans and purposes of God.

When you are given the opportunity by God, you must be ready. Saul was pleased with David and kept him at the palace.

__Psalm 75:6–7 (The Living Bible)__ [6] For promotion and power come from nowhere on earth, but only from God. He promotes one and deposes another.

What are some of the blessings and talents in your life that you need to become more skilled at? If God were to give you greater influence right now, would you be ready?

How are you using the current blessings of God in a way that stewards it properly?

What can you do right now to be faithful with what you have?

Chapter 24

Greater Influence

Nehemiah 1&2

Nehemiah was the cupbearer in the palace of King Ataxerxes, the King of Persia. Actually, he had been captured and taken to the palace, so in essence he was a slave. A cupbearer was much more than our modern "butler." It was a position of great responsibility and privilege. At each meal, he tested the king's wine to make sure it wasn't poisoned. A man who stood that close to the king in public had to be handsome, cultured, knowledgeable in court procedures, and able to converse with the king and advise him if asked. Because he had access to the king, the cupbearer was a man of great influence, which he could use for good or for evil.[6]

Sometime earlier, some Jews had returned to Jerusalem to restore the city and rebuild the walls and it seems that Nehemiah tried to keep tabs on their progress. Whenever he

---

[6] Wiersbe, W. W. (1996). *Be Determined* (p. 14). Wheaton, IL: Victor Books.

could, he would try to get info on how they were doing. On one such occasion he asked about their progress and found out that things were not going well, they were floundering. When he heard this, he sat down and cried, mourning over the news. Then he called out to God to work on their behalf. This prayer led to him asking God to grant him favor with the king so that he could go and help the people. It took four months for the opportunity to arise, but it presented itself and Nehemiah requested of the king that he be released to go and help his people rebuild the walls of Jerusalem. The king granted his request and sent him, along with resources and the appointment as the governor over the city. Nehemiah arrived there, rallied the people, and ultimately rebuilt the walls.

"If we are to have greater influence it must start with caring deeply."

There is much to learn about greater influence from this story of Nehemiah.

For us to have greater influence **we must first care enough for those we want to influence.** Nehemiah cared about the people! How do we know? Well, he actively sought out people who had returned from Israel to find out how the people in Jerusalem were doing. He wanted to know about their wellbeing. When we care for people, we want to know what is going on in their lives, we want to know that they are doing good and being successful and safe.

When Nehemiah found out about their struggles, his caring brought him to tears. He was moved with compassion for them so much so that he knew he had to do something. When we truly care then **we will do whatever is necessary**

to help those we care about. For Nehemiah that started with praying on their behalf. "O God, do something!"

A lot of times when we begin to pray for people God will call on us to partner with Him to help them, and so it was with Nehemiah that he realized that he needed to go to the people. The problem was that he was in the service of the king and to ask the king to go could end in death for him if the timing of his request was wrong. It took four months, but the opportunity arose for him to do it and he did not hesitate. He prayed and boldly asked the king to send him, and the king agreed to do so.

This is where the greater comes in...

Nehemiah obeyed God and asked the king. The king showed Nehemiah favor by sending him to go and help the people rebuild the walls. We must not be confused about how he came to care so deeply for Jerusalem. God was the one who placed the concern for Jerusalem in Nehemiah's heart. **Nehemiah nurtured that care and did something about it, and God gave the increase**. He got resources from the king and the backing of the king to do the job. He was given greater influence with the people of Jerusalem and all of it led to the people being able to rebuild the walls.

If we are to have greater influence, then it begins with us caring deeply for the things that God cares deeply about. When God sees our stewardship of that passion, He will give us favor, resources, promotions and whatever else we need to help accomplish His will in the lives of those we care for.

Who are you praying for to have greater influence with? Do you care for them? How do you show that care?

What is God asking you to do on their behalf? Are you willing to say yes?

Chapter 25

Greater Power

John 14:12 (NIV) [12] *I tell you the truth, anyone who has faith in me will do what I have been doing. He will do even greater things than these, because I am going to the Father.*

If you know that you are going to die and you had the opportunity to have a last meal with those you love, you would be very purposeful in what you share with those people right? Of all the many things that you would want to share, you would carefully curate what you said to just the important and life changing things. Jesus on the evening before his death sits with His disciples and He is sharing some final words with them and one of the things He shares with them is this gem we just read –

"I have greater power in store for you!"

We can have many discussions about what the "greater things" were that they (and us) were supposed to do, but let's not! Let's focus on the source of power who gives us the ability to do greater than we can imagine.

> *John 14:15–17 (NIV)* [15] *"If you love me, you will obey what I command.* [16] *And I will ask the Father, and he will give you another Counselor to be with you forever—* [17] *the Spirit of truth. The world cannot accept him, because it neither sees him nor knows him. But you know him, for he lives with you and will be in you.*

> *John 16:7 (NIV)* [7] *But I tell you the truth: It is for your good that I am going away. Unless I go away, the Counselor will not come to you; but if I go, I will send him to you.*

> *John 16:13 (NIV)* [13] *But when he, the Spirit of truth, comes, he will guide you into all truth. He will not speak on his own; he will speak only what he hears, and he will tell you what is yet to come.*

> *Acts 1:8 (NIV)* [8] *But you will receive power when the Holy Spirit comes on you; and you will be my witnesses in Jerusalem, and in all Judea and Samaria, and to the ends of the earth."*

Jesus tells them that they will do greater things because He has given them the power to do it – that power comes from the Holy Spirit. When they receive the Holy Spirit, they will have someone who will lead them and guide them into Greater. They will have someone who reveals greater truth to them, and He will empower them with courage and boldness to be God's witnesses wherever they go.

And that is exactly what happened.

The Holy Spirit came upon the believers, and they began to speak the Word of God boldly. They began to pray for the sick and they recovered.

They prayed for the lame and lepers, and they were healed.

They prayed for provision and God provided.

They saw those who were demon possessed freed.

They experienced greater power.

There are lots of people who will say that the miracles that are found in the book of Acts and throughout the New Testament were meant only for that time and day and they are not for today – I would disagree. Until Jesus returns for His people, our mission is to continue to be His witnesses and He has not taken away the power He gave us to be His witnesses.

"Until Jesus returns for His people, our mission is to continue to be His witnesses and He has not taken away the power He gave us to be His witnesses."

Let's consider what it means to be a witness. I imagine being a witness in a couple of word pictures. The first is being a signpost. A sign points people to something.

Los Angeles: 10 miles.

Paris: →.

Signs point people to something. As witnesses we are signposts – we are pointing people to the truth of God. We say things like, "God is powerful and in control so He can be trusted."

So, when hard times hit us and we are at peace and filled with a sense of hope and anticipation in the middle of the troubles, we are witnesses of that truth – we are signposts.

Witnesses are also people who recount what they have seen and experienced. We have experienced the love and forgiveness of God and we are to recount to others that experience. We have experienced the power of God in our own lives, and we are to recount those experiences to people and demonstrate it to them as well.

All these things require the power of the Holy Spirit.
The Holy Spirit gives us boldness to speak up.
The Holy Spirit gives us the power to pray for the sick and they recover.
The Holy Spirit gives us love, joy, peace, patience, kindness, goodness, self-control, faithfulness, and gentleness when those would not be our natural responses to the situations of life. Imagine someone being mean and vindictive to you unfairly. What is your natural response? I know for me it is to figure out a way to make them pay. Visions of revenge and making them suffer float through my head. But living in greater power means that instead of those things being my response; I act with love, joy, peace, gentleness, patience…you get the picture. That is not natural – that is supernatural, and that is the greater life that God has empowered us to live.

Last night I went to dinner with some friends and as we stopped to pray for our meal the waitress interrupted us with our salads. How rude right?! In that moment, one of the people at our table did something greater, she looked up and said,

"We are about to thank God for our food. As we pray, is there something that we can pray for you about?"

The waitress was visibly taken aback and then she replied,

"Sure, pray for me to have some deep friendships and to not feel so lonely."

We did pray for her in that moment and by itself that would be great, but there was greater Holy Spirit power at work. At the end of our meal that same person said to the waitress, "Thank you so much for your amazing service to us this evening. Would you allow me to pray for you?" Without causing a scene, without everyone bowing their heads and hollering amens, she proceeded to pray for that young lady in less than a minute. That was a greater moment! Empowered by the Holy Spirit with boldness, love, grace, and compassion, she was a witness that evening. And then she was generous in tipping the waitress. That is Holy Spirit greater at work right there.

God has empowered you for a greater work – you have been given the Holy Spirit to be His witnesses wherever you go – don't let that power go unused.

Today, ask God to use you to be His witness and demand fruit of yourself. Don't wait for something to happen. Live in the greater power that you have been given right now. Be bold and experience greater things that you have ever imagined possible.

Chapter 26

Greater Anointing

2 Kings 2:1–10 (NIV) *[1] When the* LORD *was about to take Elijah up to heaven in a whirlwind, Elijah and Elisha were on their way from Gilgal. [2] Elijah said to Elisha, "Stay here; the* LORD *has sent me to Bethel." But Elisha said, "As surely as the* LORD *lives and as you live, I will not leave you." So they went down to Bethel. [3] The company of the prophets at Bethel came out to Elisha and asked, "Do you know that the* LORD *is going to take your master from you today?" "Yes, I know," Elisha replied, "but do not speak of it." [4] Then Elijah said to him, "Stay here, Elisha; the* LORD *has sent me to Jericho." And he replied, "As surely as the* LORD *lives and as you live, I will not leave you." So they went to Jericho. [5] The company of the prophets at Jericho went up to Elisha and asked him, "Do you know that the* LORD *is going to take your master from you today?" "Yes, I know," he replied, "but do not speak of it." [6] Then Elijah said to him, "Stay*

*here; the LORD has sent me to the Jordan." And he
replied, "As surely as the LORD lives and as you
live, I will not leave you." So the two of them
walked on. ⁷ Fifty men of the company of the
prophets went and stood at a distance, facing the
place where Elijah and Elisha had stopped at the
Jordan. ⁸ Elijah took his cloak, rolled it up and
struck the water with it. The water divided to the
right and to the left, and the two of them crossed
over on dry ground. ⁹ When they had crossed,
Elijah said to Elisha, "Tell me, what can I do for
you before I am taken from you?" "Let me inherit
a double portion of your spirit," Elisha replied. ¹⁰
"You have asked a difficult thing," Elijah said, "yet
if you see me when I am taken from you, it will be
yours—otherwise not."*

The great prophet Elijah is about to be taken to heaven
and it seems that everyone knows it, including his heir-
apparent, Elisha. (Elijah and Elisha can be so easily confused
so here is how I keep them straight. J comes before S in the
alphabet, so EliJah is the first and EliSha is the second.) In
preparation for his departure Elijah decides to do a farewell
tour and visits the different schools of prophets. Elijah
encourages Elisha to stay at Bethel but Elisha refuses, he has
decided to stick to his master like food on a one-year-old. He
is a permanent fixture. And so for many miles the two of
them played a game.

"Stay here."

"Nope, I am going wherever you go."

Why did Elisha do that? Well, it seems clear that he had an
agenda. He desired a greater anointing for his life. Finally,
the moment came when Elijah knew the end was near so he

turns to his Padawan and says, "What can I do for you before I go?" The persistence has paid off and now Elisha has been asked the golden question. He didn't respond by asking for material blessings or fame, he asked for a greater anointing – a double portion of the spirit of Elijah.

> Elisha asked for a big thing – a double portion of the mighty spirit of Elijah. Elisha saw how greatly the Spirit of God worked through Elijah, and he wanted the same for himself.
> The idea of a double portion was not to ask for twice as much as Elijah had, but to ask for the portion that went to the firstborn son, as in Deuteronomy 21:17. Elisha asked for the right to be regarded as the successor of Elijah, as his firstborn son in regard to ministry. Yet Elisha had already been designated as Elijah's successor (1 Kings 19:19). This was a request for the spiritual power to fulfill the calling he already received.[7]

It is significant that Elijah's reply is that this request would be difficult to attain but could be possible only if Elisha stayed with Elijah till the end, which of course he did and was able to receive the greater anointing. I know that there is more to the anointing than miracles, but it has been observed that in his lifetime Elijah did seven great miracles and that Elisha did fourteen, many of which were the same kind of miracles such as parting the waters of the river and raising a person from the dead.

---

[7] https://enduringword.com/double-portion/ David Guzik

John 14:12–13 (NIV) [12] *I tell you the truth, anyone who has faith in me will do what I have been doing. He will do even greater things than these, because I am going to the Father.* [13] *And I will do whatever you ask in my name, so that the Son may bring glory to the Father.*

Do you realize that Jesus offers us the same thing? He offers us a greater anointing and the question is, "Do you want it?" If you do, allow me to offer a few observations from Elisha.

He desired it

Elisha wanted the double portion so much so that he was willing to do whatever it took to get it. Are we truly desirous for all of God's greater anointing on our lives or is it just words we say?

The greater anointing requires persistence and perseverance

Elijah tested Elisha. He wanted to see if he really wanted it and Elisha had to push through. Elisha didn't quit because he was tired. He didn't care if Elijah kept telling him to stay back, he was going to stick with it till he got what he desired. Remember our exploration in Luke 18 where Jesus tells the parable about persistence in prayer using the story of the widow and the judge. She didn't give up asking, she was persistent and persevering, and because of that her prayer was answered.

The greater anointing requires patience

Along with persistence and perseverance we need patience. In fact, they are inseparable. Too many of us give up too quickly because we want greater right now – and we are unwilling to go through the necessary steps to get it. Listen, it is ours to get but God takes us through a period of testing. Don't get impatient and stop following, seeking, or asking.

Greater anointing requires humility and godly character

Elisha could have asked for anything but what he did ask for was what was needed to fulfill God's purpose and call on his life – that was a sign of godly character. With great power comes great responsibility and we need humility and godly character to be able to handle it. Only after Elisha demonstrates his loyalty and commitment is he offered the chance to get more. We need to handle well what we have to show that we can handle more.

We should all desire greater anointing. I want all that God has for me, but the motivation should be the same as that of Jesus when He spoke of Greater in John 14…"so that it brings glory to the Father."

And the last thing is probably the most obvious…
If you want a greater anointing – ask for it!

> ***Matthew 7:7–8 (NIV)*** *[7] "Ask and it will be given to you; seek and you will find; knock and the door will be opened to you. [8] For everyone who asks receives; he who seeks finds; and to him who knocks, the door will be opened.*

So…do you want it?

Chapter 27

Greater Is Always Tied To Obedience

Exodus 14:5–31 (NIV) *[5] When the king of Egypt was told that the people had fled, Pharaoh and his officials changed their minds about them and said, "What have we done? We have let the Israelites go and have lost their services!" [6] So he had his chariot made ready and took his army with him. [7] He took six hundred of the best chariots, along with all the other chariots of Egypt, with officers over all of them. [8] The LORD hardened the heart of Pharaoh king of Egypt, so that he pursued the Israelites, who were marching out boldly. [9] The Egyptians—all Pharaoh's horses and chariots, horsemen and troops—pursued the Israelites and overtook them as they camped by the sea near Pi Hahiroth, opposite Baal Zephon. [10] As Pharaoh approached, the Israelites looked up, and there were the Egyptians, marching after them. They were terrified and cried out to the LORD. [11] They said to*

Moses, "Was it because there were no graves in Egypt that you brought us to the desert to die? What have you done to us by bringing us out of Egypt? [12] Didn't we say to you in Egypt, 'Leave us alone; let us serve the Egyptians'? It would have been better for us to serve the Egyptians than to die in the desert!" [13] Moses answered the people, "Do not be afraid. Stand firm and you will see the deliverance the LORD will bring you today. The Egyptians you see today you will never see again. [14] The LORD will fight for you; you need only to be still." [15] Then the LORD said to Moses, "Why are you crying out to me? Tell the Israelites to move on. [16] Raise your staff and stretch out your hand over the sea to divide the water so that the Israelites can go through the sea on dry ground. [17] I will harden the hearts of the Egyptians so that they will go in after them. And I will gain glory through Pharaoh and all his army, through his chariots and his horsemen. [18] The Egyptians will know that I am the LORD when I gain glory through Pharaoh, his chariots and his horsemen." [19] Then the angel of God, who had been traveling in front of Israel's army, withdrew and went behind them. The pillar of cloud also moved from in front and stood behind them, [20] coming between the armies of Egypt and Israel. Throughout the night the cloud brought darkness to the one side and light to the other side; so neither went near the other all night long. [21] Then Moses stretched out his hand over the sea, and all that night the LORD drove the sea back with a strong east wind and turned it into dry land. The

*waters were divided, 22 and the Israelites went
through the sea on dry ground, with a wall of
water on their right and on their left. 23 The
Egyptians pursued them, and all Pharaoh's horses
and chariots and horsemen followed them into
the sea. 24 During the last watch of the night the
LORD looked down from the pillar of fire and cloud
at the Egyptian army and threw it into confusion.
25 He made the wheels of their chariots come off
so that they had difficulty driving. And the
Egyptians said, "Let's get away from the
Israelites! The LORD is fighting for them against
Egypt."*

---

*"We want God to take us out of the situations,
but He wants to take us through!"*

---

*26 Then the LORD said to Moses, "Stretch out your
hand over the sea so that the waters may flow
back over the Egyptians and their chariots and
horsemen." 27 Moses stretched out his hand over
the sea, and at daybreak the sea went back to its
place. The Egyptians were fleeing toward it, and
the LORD swept them into the sea. 28 The water
flowed back and covered the chariots and
horsemen—the entire army of Pharaoh that had
followed the Israelites into the sea. Not one of
them survived. 29 But the Israelites went through
the sea on dry ground, with a wall of water on
their right and on their left. 30 That day the LORD
saved Israel from the hands of the Egyptians, and
Israel saw the Egyptians lying dead on the shore.
31 And when the Israelites saw the great power
the LORD displayed against the Egyptians, the*

*people feared the LORD and put their trust in him
and in Moses his servant.*

Moses is struggling for people to trust him. He has been called by God to help set them free, something that they had been crying out to God for. Moses had been courageous enough to come and stand up to the Pharaoh, but the people are fickle. They are going with Moses, but should a better option come along then it is adios Moses.

After some tense negotiations the Pharaoh had let the Israelites go. Very soon thereafter he changes his mind and sets off after them with his army – the entire army. This is not a peace-keeping op.

God has directed Moses in what seems like a losing strategy. They are camped in a place that locked them in from any escape from Pharaoh. In front of them is the sea, on the sides are mountains and behind them, bearing down on them, is the Egyptian army. The people begin to panic and as people do when they are faced with danger or hardship, they look for someone to blame and Moses is the one who is going to be their fall guy. Emotions are running high, and Moses is in danger of being strung up.

This is a tough situation for Moses to be in. The stress is unbelievable. He has told these people that after hundreds of years of slavery they are going to be free and he has led them out, but now the old master is bearing down on them. What makes it worse it that Moses knows that the Pharaoh is going to make an example of them so that he could re-enslave them through fear and intimidation. Moses goes to God complaining. Wouldn't you? You obeyed God and now He has placed you in a terrible situation. All these people are looking at you and saying,

"You got us into this situation. This is your fault that we are going to die."

I am pretty sure that their solution to the problem was to surrender quickly to Pharaoh and hope for the best.

Have you ever felt that way? You are feeling the stress of others depending on you. You have made decisions that affect their future and instead of it going well it seems to have gone sideways. Everything is falling apart, and they are getting ready to string you up – and honestly you feel like that would be the best option at this time.

Moses goes to God and God's response is,
"Quit yer whining and keep moving forward."
"Ummm but God, I am not sure you notice that we cannot move forward, there is an ocean in the way, and I don't see that we have enough boats to get everyone across."
"Boats? Boats? We don't need no stinking boats. Raise your staff and stretch your hand over the sea to divide the water and the people will walk through the middle of the sea on dry land."

Come on, does that seem like the answer anyone under stress to produce something now would want to hear?
"God, change the mind of the Pharaoh."
"Let there be a rockslide that cuts off the Egyptian army from getting to the Israelites."

Those solutions sound plausible – but raise your staff and your hand and divide the sea down the middle? If I am Moses, I would have had a heart to heart with God right there.
"OK boss, I told you I didn't want this job, but you convinced me to do it and told me that you would handle the details. This does not look like you are handling the details, and if we even get out of this situation, the people are going to revolt against me. I quit!"

Thankfully Moses does not quit – he went for Greater. He chose to look foolish in front of thousands of people and obeyed God. He raised his staff and stretched out his hand and because of his obedience, God went to work. The sea parted overnight and the next day the people were able to walk through on dry land. I imagine it as the first Sea World! Water walled up on either side, people looking in and seeing the fishes. "Hey, there is Shamu!" All right I know it was not like that, but I can have some fun imagining.

When the Israelites passed through, God allowed the Egyptian army to follow. It seemed like God's answer, though miraculous, was not going to be the answer. The Egyptian army followed onto the sea floor and just when it looked like capture was imminent the sea came back together and completely engulfed the army and they were all destroyed. God did the impossible.

Stop for a moment and think about it. God could have done it all without Moses, but He worked in partnership with Moses. God instructed Moses to do something that looked dumb and counterproductive. With an army bearing down on them to do bodily harm and enslave them, God's answer was for Moses to raise his staff and arm with the intent of parting the sea. That was crazy and without precedence. Moses was under pressure from people to "do something," but what God told him to do did not seem like the action that would fill the people with trust for God or Moses. Yet in that very stressful moment Moses chose trust and obedience and God came through for him.

Moses is no different than us. He was feeling the stress and panic – but he chose to obey, and that obedience led to Greater. Look at verse 31 again...

³¹ And when the Israelites saw the great power the LORD displayed against the Egyptians, the people feared the LORD and put their trust in him and in Moses his servant.

Moses experienced greater influence because he was obedient to God regardless of how crazy the instructions from God had sounded. This is where the Greater happens. Only after the obedience of Moses did the amazing miracle take place. He got past his doubts and fears and chose to obey God and not give in to the crowd.

Too many of us are missing our Greater moments because we are afraid to say yes to God. We are afraid to give out of our need. We are afraid to step out of our comfort zone. We are afraid to look stupid. We are afraid to speak God's confirming word to a stranger. And so, we miss out. We miss out on the Greater.

There is a greater future that God wants for you. He wants you to experience greater intimacy, greater insight, greater increase, and greater influence if you would trust and obey! Let's get to it!

Choose Greater!

About the Author

 Gary Khan was born on the island of Trinidad in the Caribbean. He moved to America when he was 20 to pursue his education and calling to be a pastor. He met his wife DeLaine at Eugene Bible College (now New Hope Christian College) and upon their graduation (June 1990), they were married and began working at Desert Streams Church in Santa Clarita, CA. They are still pastors at Desert Streams Church. Gary and DeLaine are the proud parents of Ethan and Allison and so many others that they consider their spiritual sons and daughters.

Gary's joy and passion is discipling people and helping them to be made more in the image and likeness of Jesus.

I hope you have enjoyed this 28-day spiritual challenge; I had a great time writing it and I pray that it has been a blessing to you. If you have found this book helpful and enjoyable, check out my other devotionals on Amazon. You can also check my Facebook page *https://www.facebook.com/GaryFVKhan* for details and while you're there click on the Follow button to get updates on other devotionals and books.

Made in the USA
Coppell, TX
23 November 2021

66283176R00079